IN A WORLD

HOW TO MAKE BOOK TRAILERS THAT SELL MORE BOOKS

BY:

RICHARD BAILEY

TABLE OF CONTENTS

IN A WORLD where book trailers are laughably poor quality, cheesy, ugly, nigh-unwatchable; dare to create something that stands above the rest.

IN A WORLD of skyrocketing costs and expensive-sounding expertise, promote your novel without spending any money.

IN A WORLD where every other author appears to be rich and successful, have the tenacity to make them all jealous.

These are the secrets to creating something that excites people about your book.

Something bold.

Something beautiful.

Something that will help you actually *sell more books*.

THIS IS YOUR QUINTESSENTIAL GUIDE TO MAKING BOOK TRAILERS YOU CAN ACTUALLY AFFORD.

WHO AM I TO SAY SO?

True, there is already information out there about how to make book trailers and promote the sale of books. Not much of it is cohesive, easy to find, or high-quality, but like everything on the internet, if you look hard enough you can find *something*. Usually, it's a brief blog article or sales pitch telling you how to make a low-quality book trailer...and that's kind of it. Not a deep discussion of techniques, not a manual that teaches you video "grammar," not an in-depth look at what to do with it all once you've finally created this video masterpiece that talks about your book.

What you're likely looking for is an explanation of how you—an unknown author with, let's say, *limited* funds—can make a video, get it "out there" and then use that video as a way to sell books. You know there's a way to use moving images to get audiences interested in your book. And you're hoping there's something that can help you learn how to do that.

Most of this invaluable how-to information is authored by, well, authors. Writers. Experts in their field, to be sure. But they're experts at *writing,* not video production. The two skills are intertwined, but often authors talking about video production approach the process in terms of the written, as opposed to the visual. This leaves most of their audience with several rather large holes in their expertise when it comes to making visual advertisements for their books. Those holes result in missed opportunities to grow platforms, gain readers, and sell many, many more books.

I think there's a different way to approach book trailers, and that's why I'm writing this. Along with being a novelist, I am a film producer, director, and editor.

I'm constantly using the power of moving images to communicate ideas and sell products. And make no mistake; your book is a *product*. It is made with love and time; devotion and wit; sacrifice and bravery. It is certainly more than a widget you've mass-produced. It is a unique slice of your talent and your soul. But at the end of the day it's still something you hope to expose audiences to. It is art, but most likely it's art you'd like to make money off of.

Products need to be promoted, marketed, and advertised for. That's what I specialize in. Over the past decade I've written, shot, edited, and produced thousands of videos for hundreds of clients and earned millions of views. These projects run the gambit from feature films to short films, commercials to sales videos, training videos to product promos, documentaries to, of course, book trailers. I've analyzed and critiqued trailers, films, demo reels, and commercials, and to date I've won over 50 industry awards for projects of all kinds.

I've learned a few tricks along the way, and I want to share the intimate, in-depth details of creating a book trailer with authors.

As an author myself I understand the world and the mind of a writer (insofar as there *is* anything at all comprehensible about an writer's mind...). As a video producer I understand the needs of a production. I want to combine both sides of the coin: the written side and the visual side. I don't believe these two sides are at odds with each other.

So I encourage you to soak up this knowledge I've gained from my experiences, successes, and mistakes. It is my sincere hope you'll gain some valuable, unique insight from my particular perspectives.

And maybe have a little fun, too.

CHAOS & COMPETITION: E-COMMERCE AT ITS FINEST

The world is in chaos, even if you don't know it. The internet has broken the sound barrier when it comes to communication, technological advancements, and instant gratification. Today we expect *everything* to happen *immediately*. Honestly, when was the last time you waited more than five seconds for something to load without doing something else to distract you? We're so impatient we've created apps for you to pre-order *fast food!*

And, to top it all off, there's now an endless population of writers, authors, bloggers, "influencers," tinkerers, and pontificators all vying for an audience. And somehow they're all making *money* doing this. They're selling their products to the great e-beyond, and you're hoping to join their ranks by selling your book online—whether you're self-published, working with a small publishing house, or you've seduced The Big Five.

It's a global food fight with constantly changing rules. Everyone from big publishers to independent authors are confused and competing online, and that means the old barriers to publishing, marketing, and finding an audience for your book have disintegrated. Welcome to the Thunderdome.

In order to stand out and pull in readers, you need a product worth buzzing about. Not only does the content of your book need to rock, but the way new readers *find* that content is just as important. And one thing's clear in this brave new world of e-commerce: it's not just about good writing. It's about presentation.

Which is why to help you sell books, you need to create video. This is often called a book trailer.

Okay, stop hyperventilating and let me elaborate.

With the continued explosion and expansion of the internet and all things webby, the use of video has become overwhelmingly popular. And it just keeps growing. As more people around the world begin performing every imaginable function online, the way in which we communicate is evolving. Some circles even believe humanity is moving away from a written-communication-based society back to an oral and visual society. All of this is thanks to video: you no longer need to read all those pesky *words*, you can just watch someone say them.

So Why Write a Book?

Don't get me wrong: I am not under the impression that the written word will be extinct in the next 50 years, and you shouldn't be, either. Otherwise there'd be no reason to write this very book. I could probably make a pretty good case that we will communicate in completely new and nearly incomprehensible ways, but being able to put our thoughts into words will never, ever be irrelevant.

Whatever the language, the written word is here to stay. It is a very strong, very personal, very subjective way to communicate—even moreso than video. Reading allows audiences to imagine greater, to create pictures in their minds; something a photograph or video could never do, no matter how big the budget.

Which means that though the platform changes, the need for books—sci-fi, romance, horror, comedy, thriller, mystery, informational, argumentative, revolutionary, or any other type—will never become extinct. In fact, as we begin to lose our way and a little bit of ourselves through all of the exponentially growing instant communication chaos, long works of literature will become even more important to keeping us sane.

We are beginning to see a little bit of this now, as the popularity of e-publishing, self-publishing, and digital bookstores continues to rise. People want an escape from the insta-everything.

But how do they choose this escape? Where do they shop for their next written adventure? On the internet, of course. That fickle, slippery beast that everyone loves and loathes simultaneously.

Harnessing the Power of the Internet

It is easier than ever for someone to write something and release it to a global audience. The problem is, of course, that it's easier than ever for *anyone* to write something and release it to a global audience. The market is flooded with authors struggling to grab the attention of a large audience, and this makes it an incredibly competitive world for writers and an overwhelming world for readers.

As an author with so much competition out there, making your book stand out is like trying to yell the loudest in Times Square on New Year's Eve—you'd better have a pretty big megaphone.

Our goal as authors and marketers should be to solve our reader's main problem—wading through the noise to find what they *want* to read. Make sure that megaphone is telling them what they need to know.

Currently the best way to obtain and wield said megaphone is through an online platform, search engine optimization (SEO), hooking up with local bookstores, blogging and commenting and keywording and tweeting, Facebooking, Instagramming, Tumblring, Good Reads-ing, and loads and loads of other wibbly-wobbly-webby things. By the time you read this all of those things may be distant memories of a simpler time gone by. Even big traditional publishers depend on authors to do their own marketing, so don't expect that contract with the Big Five to solve your discoverability crisis.

And this is all to catch the eye of *potential* readers. Don't forget you actually have to have something excellent to show them! And the hardest part is...*everyone* is competing in the same way.

So how do you stand out from this crowd? How do you harness the power of video on the internet to help draw readers to your writing?

Make a movie trailer. For your book.

A BOOK...TRAILER? WHY?

Most people look at you cross-eyed when you say you've created a "book trailer". What is it for? Why? People often tell me that they want to *read* a book, not watch it. They don't even know what to think of the idea. "So, it's a movie trailer...for a book?" It doesn't make sense. Then again, neither does a television commercial talking about the taste of gum. But the goal is the same; it's all about connecting with the audience, baby. You're not just selling the features of your product, be they words or a minty fresh taste. You're selling the benefits, you're selling the idea, you're selling the *experience*.

Trailers make money. They work. There are trailers for movies, television shows, video games, live events, and just about any other type of storytelling medium. But still not many for books. Why is that?

A Rose by Any Other Name

First of all, the term "book trailer" is a misnomer. It's actually a **book video**. This distinction is important, because I want you to think of it not as a traditional movie trailer, but as a *commercial* for your book. A marketing tool that helps readers find your work, and helps money flow from audiences to you. Call it a commercial, a trailer, a teaser, a documentary, a promo, or anything else, it's all the same thing. The danger of thinking in terms of a book "trailer" is people often assume a *book* trailer should feel like a *movie* trailer. This leads to limitations and problems.

It also conjures up thoughts of the scores of poorly-produced, low-budget, amateur video "book trailers" which, collectively, have created a stigma that *all* book trailers are as abysmal as these cheap, tacky, inartistic dumpster fires that run rampant throughout the internet.

When you think of a book trailer, it's this lowbrow type of video you probably think of. And because that's currently the most prevalent form of video advertisement for books, you probably assume all book trailers are ineffective, money-sucking heaps reserved for the illiterate masses with no taste.

This stigma is pervasive, and calling something a book trailer is often a death sentence when authors think of ways to market their books. Trailers are for morons, not intelligent people who read books, right? Trailers are flashy but without substance, you say. Trailers are limiting, because you wrote a *book*, not a *movie*, darn it.

Instead, if you think of your work as a book *commercial*, all types of styles and opportunities open up to you. You'll see me often use the term "book video" interchangeably with "book trailer," because it doesn't come with the same cultural baggage. No matter what you call it, you want to create compelling content that ensnares your audience, kidnaps their attention, and punches them right in the feels.

Your Main Goal with Video

I am a film and video producer, and I work with clients of all types—most of whom know close to nothing about video production. And they don't have to. There's only one goal when it comes to marketing anything with video, particularly with books: *show the audience why they need the product*.

Try to capture the emotions your audience will feel, try to *show* them, rather than tell them, what they will gain from reading your book. This doesn't have to be literally articulated. I don't suggest you appear in front of the camera, deer-in-the-headlights stare plastered to your face and say, "my...uh...n-novel will excite you. It has a-adventure, romance, and, uh, giant space s-s-spiders. Yeah. Space Spiders. Uh. Please buy my book."

You want something engaging, something that will grab audiences and make them think *I have got to get this book right now*. Every reader has needs, whether they're entertainment needs or informational needs. You want something that can succinctly tell them that, if they buy your book, those needs will be met.

Okay, but Why?

Hollywood figured it out a long time ago. Film companies learned that excitement for a story will net many more ticket sales. A good trailer sells a lot of tickets because it foments audience awareness and intrigue without giving too much away. The same can be true of your book. People simply *have to see that story* if the trailer is good enough. This fact, combined with widespread sharing of exciting content on the internet, means today trailers are more important than ever.

There's no shortage of ridiculous statistics about how many people use the web to consume video content. Over 100 million videos are viewed every day on the internet. And only half of those are cat videos. That shows you the power of video. Why not harness that power to help get the word out about your book?

Readers go to online outlets to buy their books. Right now we have Amazon, Kindle, Barnes and Noble, iBooks, and any number of other sites that sell e-books. Chances are in the next few years there will be many, many more online retailers. Today, e-books make up around 50% of all books purchased, and that's a conservative estimate. Closer to 90% of all romance books purchased are ebooks, and roughly 75% of science fiction and fantasy[1].

As a reader, when you visit one of these sites to buy a book, you can click on the title, author, or book cover image to get to the book's sales page. This page has all sorts of useful information, such as the book cover photo, information about the author, other books by the same author, other similar

---

[1] GeekWire.com – Frank Catalano "Traditional publishers'

books, ratings, comments, and of course the text telling readers what the book is about (we'll call this the *blurb*). What if, on this page, you could also click on a one-minute video? Most people would decide whether or not to buy the book based primarily—if not solely—on whatever is in that video. How much faster and easier would it be for you to pick and purchase a book this way? How much more likely would you be to impulse buy that book if the video was good?

Statistics show that, contrary to what they might tell you in public, most readers would much rather watch a video than read all those extraneous, salesy, black-and-white words. *Even if they want to read the book.* Therefore it behooves you to give them what they want, create a video and make it easier for them to fall in love with your previously unheard-of book.

If you don't believe me, try it yourself. Make two web pages: one with a video, the other with words. The content for each page must be the same, so the video should be a visual representation of what the words say. Get out your fancy web analytics and tell me which page gets more viewers, and which one retains those viewers longer. I guarantee you it's the page with the video. Somewhere between 70-80% of people on the web watch video before reading *a single word of text*.

Use this to your advantage.

As an Independent Author

Chances are you're self-publishing. It's better for royalties, it gives you more control, and it's easier than ever these days. In addition to just promoting your book on the sales page, you need to build and grow your platform.

You're likely developing that platform with all sorts of websites, articles, email lists, and social media posts. You're attending writer's conventions and meeting local bookstore owners. You're in charge of your own marketing campaign. Most importantly, you want a way to pull in readers without them feeling like they're being sold to. You also need *content* to share on your platform, to excite your email, YouTube, Facebook, Twitter, and Instagram followers. You want to sell books to those folks who just didn't want to read your blurb. You want your book—and yourself—to be visible in more places online, driving more traffic to your website.

You'll also want to develop a platform in person. All of those conferences and seminars you're attending, all of those happy hours and book signings, all of those networking events and promotional get-to-know-the-author events are perfect places to stand out from others. Perfect places to meet new readers who will get excited about your work. You'll need to cultivate those real-world audiences.

Think of a book trailer as a way to do all of this and more. Video is one of the world's most powerful tools. Use it, and you'll sell more. Easier.

Seducing Publishers

Say you're taking the traditional publishing route, querying agents and editors. You've put together a stellar query letter, your synopsis is perfectly paced, and those first three chapters are so good you should frame them. This should make you a sure-fire selection for the agent, but thirty queries later, you're still agent-less. And hearing about all of those now-famous and rich authors who were rejected hundreds of times before being published doesn't quite keep you smiling. In fact, it just makes you feel miserable. If J.K. Rowling had to query 250 agents before more or less *accidentally* getting discovered by a publisher, how many agents do *you* have to query? Why, oh why, didn't you just get a job as an insurance adjuster?

Give yourself time to sober up, and start thinking about what you can do to get ahead of the pack. Maybe you need something to help you stand out. You're looking for a different vehicle to show off your *writing skillz* and prove that you know how to market a book. Or maybe you're looking for an innovative way to introduce yourself to agents or make a case for your expertise.

In these situations a book video makes a lot of sense, even for a book that *has not been published* (we'll get into what type of book video this should be later).

An agent, editor, or publisher has essentially the same need you have when looking for a quick book to buy—she needs to feel a connection with the book and its author. She needs to know that this book will make her some friggin' *money*. And the trailer should be designed to show that. It is a promise to readers, agents, editors, and publishers that they will be entertained or enlightened by these scribbled words. You want to create something that will not only tell people about the book, but *show* them. Something that will elicit a visceral reaction, let them know they will *feel* something.

Because ultimately that's why we, as audience members, seek out entertainment. Books, movies, TV shows, music, and art of any kind appeals to our emotions. A video is by no means a substitute to a query letter, but it helps show off how exciting the book is, what readers will learn or enjoy, where the adventure will take them. It promises their needs will be met.

Less-Than-Obvious Reasons

Another advantage of a book trailer is that it doubles as an uncanny icebreaker. Never have anything exciting to say at those writing conferences or awful networking events? This is a great way to show something unique and entertaining.

I once showed my book trailer to an agent at a conference and her mouth fell open. "I...I've never seen anything like this before," she said. And this opened a door that eventually led to her requesting the manuscript. I stood out from the crowd in a memorable way. Otherwise I'd just have to rely on my good looks and charm...in which case I would be hosed.

It's also a great way to prove you can write. If you can create something engaging with a one-minute video, chances are you can write a pretty good story.

The cool thing about this is that if you're smart enough, you can create this piece of work for almost zero cost to you.

And it's not as hard as you might think.

BUT...UH...WHAT THE HECK *IS* A BOOK TRAILER?

In its most basic form, a book trailer is a video somewhere between 30 seconds and two minutes that creates interest for the content of your book. This can be a dramatic video in the style of a movie trailer, or an informational video, an author interview, a teaser, a cartoon, a commercial, or even a music video. Ultimately the type of trailer you want to create is up to you. What you do to show people that your book is worth reading depends only on the limits of your creativity, your ingenuity, and your talent.

Okay, you're on board so far, but maybe you know as much about video production as I do about performing simian neurosurgery in space. That's okay. The mechanics of production is what this little book is here to help you with.

But let's be honest, you've seen the book trailers out there. Many are laughably poor quality and only have 37 views. Bad voice-over audio, poor pacing, grainy images or mismatching still photos, and enough cheese to fill a pizza parlor. Not exactly Spielberg. We've all seen these, and most people associate those types of videos with book trailers as a whole. Let's change that.

Because, again, you're not trying to poorly mimic a movie trailer. You're trying to make a **commercial** for your book. You're trying to sell a **product**. You want to avoid something cringe-worthy and low quality, and make something that will have people clambering over one another to buy your book. I genuinely believe you can.

Everyone today claims they can shoot a video on their phone, but I'm talking about *professional-level* video. Usually that means a nice camera, lights, actors, crew, sound, graphics, and the whole dog and pony show. There's a reason it costs $100 million to shoot a three-hour Hollywood movie. If you have that kind of cash, this book isn't for you—go hire a high-dollar professional team (like mine!) and just go ahead and turn your book *into* a movie.

For everyone else, let's learn a few free tricks to take your book trailer out of amateur hour. Video production doesn't need to be complicated or expensive. In fact, I'll walk you through how to do the things you need to do in order to make a book-selling video. You'll be surprised what you can do with limited cash and just a little professional knowledge.

Know What You Want

Whether you're making home movies or Hollywood epics, the most important part about any type of video production is ***knowing what you want***. In this case, you want an advertisement for your book. There are millions of different ways to do this, and I don't think you want to read something that outlines even half of those. But there are standards and rules that you'd be wise to learn and master.

The book video in its most basic form is a tool to pique interest for your book. It's not one-size-fits-all. Yes, your book video can be a dramatic trailer, in the style of a Hollywood epic. You can have actors and sets and explosions and the whole nine yards. This may not be relevant to your book, however—or your wallet.

Say you've got an informational non-fiction book about banana peeling techniques. In that case, your video should discuss the problem readers have, namely improper banana peeling etiquette, and how reading the book will help them solve their problem. No explosions needed.

Perhaps you have an academic treatise about avocados, and the best way to spark interest for the book is by getting on-camera testimonials from some avocado experts in the field.

Or maybe you can explain your great science fiction trilogy through flying text and dramatic music, because, well, you don't have any way to film an alien 50 million light years away that only exists inside a black hole.

Just as the topics vary, so does the style of video. Tell your story through moving text, or cartoons, or interviews. You can make a funny commercial, or recreate a dramatic scene, or even speak directly to the audience on camera. The possibilities, as they say, are endless. Even if you've written a book about making book videos, you can make a book video about that book! I can't tell you what is best for your book, but I *can* tell you how to do it. I can recommend some good places to start—and some great places to end up.

The Most Important Questions

The most important part about crafting your book video is to develop a creative approach that sells your story. For almost any type of fictional work, your book video should answer three simple questions:

1. **Who is the main character?** - *This can be the good guy and/or bad guy (protagonist and antagonist for you proper folks), but this person must be compelling and we must understand why we would root for/against them. If the protagonist is a group (i.e. "The X-Men"), it is still best to focus on one person as the main character (i.e. Wolverine is the protagonist in "X-Men").*

2. **What does he/she want?** - *In other words, what is their goal and what is at stake? The more compelling this motivation is, the more you're likely to get people rooting for your hero. Your goal is to try to make this goal as specific as possible. "Save the world" isn't a specific goal, but, "save the world from flesh-eating space slugs using nothing but toothpicks" creates all kinds of interest. This isn't a perfect example (do the slugs use toothpicks, or do you?), but you get the idea. Be specific.*

3. **What is standing in the way?** - *This may either be the main conflict, the main opponent, or a combination of both. It's important*

to establish this in order to show audiences that something will happen in the story, that the reader will feel a sense of accomplishment or failure (some type of emotion) not to be gathered elsewhere. In many cases, the conflict is what makes the story so interesting. You shouldn't have a hero if they didn't overcome great odds.

Even if you're writing non-fiction, these questions still apply. Memoirs, investigations, and histories should be able to answer the above questions in some form or another. However, there are books that don't have a protagonist/antagonist, such as how-to books (like this one), descriptive or encyclopedic (a classification of dinosaur fossils, for example), or art books (a collection of M.C. Escher drawings and photographs).

Although these topics don't lend themselves directly to explosions, car chases, and beautiful people falling in love, you can still make a damn good commercial for any of them. No matter what it's about, you must still show us why your book is worth buying. To do so, ask yourself these questions:

1. **What problem exists?** - *This can either be a universal problem such as poor education, or a specific problem for a specific audience, such as mothers trying to educate ADHD children. The problem may also be a bit indirect or hard to figure out, but I promise it's there. For example, what is the problem that a dinosaur fossil classification book solves?* Lack of education about dinosaur fossil classification! *That's not very sexy, nor is it very specific. And the more specific this problem, the more engaging your video (and your writing) is likely to be. For our dinosaur bones book, perhaps the problem really is* lack of knowledge of dinosaur fossil classification has lead to incorrect theories of evolution and extinction. *Now you've got some stakes implied: if you misclassify dinosaur bones, you may go extinct!*

2. **What or how does this book propose to solve/treat this problem?** - *Here is the heart of your approach; the reason people are paying for your knowledge. Tell them how your book will help them. Again, with our dinosaur example, you can tell the audience that the book will teach you the way to properly identify and classify dinosaur bones, thus shedding new light on a groundbreaking theory of evolution. This works to also serve as a "hook" for your audience. Something that they will be curious about, something that gets them saying, "There's a new theory of evolution?? What? I must know!"*

3. **Why is this book different than other books of the same kind?** - *Say there are already several books about the classification of dinosaur fossils. It's a good idea to be able to tell readers why your book is better than anyone else's. You don't have to be snotty about it—in fact, it's a terrible idea to trash other's work—but you should certainly have a unique take on the subject, a new theory or*

discovery, or input from an expert in the field. For our dinosaur fossil book, we'll definitely want to mention that the book contains a new theory of evolution, and also that we've amassed research and testimonials from a strong, expert, previously unknown (or untapped) source. In this case, let's say the findings from a newly discovered dig in the Montana flatlands and the opinions of the world's leading paleontologist. That means no one else is saying the same thing you are; your book is unique and important.

4. **What are the author's credentials?** - *Why the heck should I believe you? This may be more important for some topics than others, but it never hurts to let your audience know that you know what you're talking about. Are you, the author, an expert in your field? Have you studied the topic for years and years, or been praised by critics for your contributions to the industry? Maybe you were friends with someone who was otherwise inaccessible, making you the best person to tell their story. Or since you're an artist yourself, you have the knowledge to pick out the best artwork of the year. Perhaps you're the evolutionary paleontologist who is on the cutting edge of dinosaur fossil classification. The point is to impress upon the reader that by listening to you (er...reading you...) they will get something unique and—hopefully—better than they can get anywhere else in the world.*

For both fiction and nonfiction, these important questions should look awfully familiar. These are the same types of questions you'd likely address in a query letter, synopsis, summary, or any way that you talk about your book. That's because you'll want your video to be consistent with the rest of your marketing, and your marketing to be consistent with the experience of reading your book. You wouldn't want your video to feel like a horror movie trailer, your blurb to sound like a romance, and your actual book to read like a history. Those feelings don't mesh, and someone who watches your book video and really likes it is going to be very disappointed—and possibly leave a bad review—if your book doesn't live up to the promise made by your marketing material.

And although answering these questions is the goal of your book video, you shouldn't answer them overtly in the same way you don't want your main character to just *say* the theme of your novel. Try to make these answers subtle and organic.

You'll also notice answering these questions doesn't require you to give away hardly anything about the plot itself. A trailer is a tease. It's a seduction. The less actual story you can give away, the better. You just have to carefully walk that fine line between letting the audience know enough to get excited about your story, and giving away too much.

Creativity is Fluid

Before we get ahead of ourselves, I want to dispel you of the notion that these rules are ironclad. *Nothing* in the creative world is set in stone, or even sand, so yes; there are ways to approach making a book video that have nothing to do with answering these questions. I would bet, however, that if you looked at the best ones hard enough, you could see they answer these questions without even trying.

It's also important to know you can answer these questions in incredibly creative ways. In the same way no one can tell you how to be an excellent writer, so too can no one teach you to make the video that is right for *your* book—you've just got to do it. These ideas that I'm giving you are neon anchor lines to guide you through the darkest part of the ocean. I can't swim for you. But I firmly believe that if you are creative and passionate, you can learn these basics, expand upon them, and create something truly marvelous.

It's been a while since I've had my socks blown off, and I'm hoping to arm you with the necessary stocking explosives to do just that.

TYPES OF BOOK VIDEOS

The cool thing about video is that there's really no way to do it wrong—unless you're using your cell phone to film your cat. There are already millions of these videos out there, and seriously, how many cat videos does the world need??

Other than that, video gives you the opportunity to say *anything you want*. You can scare people, or educate them, inspire them or show them the inescapable bond of true love. It just depends on how you want to tell your story. And make no mistake; video is just like writing in that way—at the end of the day, it's all about the *story*.

And just like a book, there are different ways to tell that story.

Dramatic Trailer

Probably the most common book video is the dramatic book trailer. By this I mean something that looks and feels much like a movie trailer. The dramatic trailer features either a voice over artist ("*In a world where hope is outlawed...*"), graphic text that appears on the screen (**IN A WORLD WHERE HOPE IS OUTLAWED**...), one of the characters narrating (*"My name is Naomi, and I live in a world where hope is outlawed..."*), or some combination of the three. This is all tied together with driving music and sound effects.

Visually, the dramatic trailer features images from scenes that would plausibly appear in the book. For example, if you have a fictional story about a murderer burying a body in the mud, you're likely to include footage of an actor digging a grave in the mud. An advantage is that you don't have to film a whole scene like a movie. Sometimes merely one shot (in other words, one *image*) can get across the look and feel of what you're going for.

You'll also potentially feature clips from different scenes in your book, whether it be characters performing actions like digging, running, driving, shooting, kissing, or whatever; or characters speaking and acting out scenes from the book, including dialogue. Think of that movie trailer where Arnold yells, "Get to the chopper!" or Jack screams, "You can't handle the truth!" You'll want little clips like this in your trailer if you want to make it feel dramatic and real. Maybe pick one or two of the most telling, most dramatic exclamations your characters say, and throw those into the mix.

Most dramatic trailers use a little bit of everything, and mix it all together into a montage that answers those three important questions through narration, text, dialogue, and action. Again, for review, let's see those three questions:

1. Who is the main character?

2. What does he/she want?

3. What is standing in the way?

The style and amount of shots and scenes you use depends entirely on what you've written, how you've developed your creative approach, and what you believe best tells the story. Just remember that your trailer should be a tease, not a re-telling, of your story. You want to entice people, so don't give away any spoilers!

And you don't even need to have *footage* to call something a dramatic trailer. Perhaps you have some animation skills, or know a cartoonist. The movie trailer format works just as well, no matter your artistic approach. So long as it feels like a movie trailer in that it is written, paced, and edited to evoke high emotion.

If you're still not clear on what I mean by a dramatic trailer, open up your handy dandy web browser and search for "movie trailers". Hundreds and hundreds of dramatic trailers should be readily available for you to look over. Pick a few that you like and a few that look similar to your story. Take notes on their styles and what keeps you interested, and try to pick a style that might work with your book.

If you've heard the phrase, "steal like an artist," you should. Use work that you love to inspire work that you create. Just don't infringe on someone's copyright.

The Teaser

This is a sub-section of the dramatic trailer, but bears its own explanation. To many people, the idea of a trailer for a book that looks like a trailer for a film is almost certainly blasphemy. Sometimes the idea of seeing people when the reader of their book should be *imagining* people is categorically offensive. Sometimes a full-blown dramatic scenario would simply ruin the book. Sometimes the book takes place in a situation that is completely infeasible to shoot. Whatever the reason, there is another way to copy movie trailers without giving away hardly anything. This is called 'the teaser'.

This trailer only pretends to be a dramatic scenario. When you break it down, it gives away nothing of substance about the book. It just *teases* the audience, hence the name.

Think of a superhero movie reveal. We see the silhouette of a woman, darkly lit over a dark background. The character narrates off screen, saying, *"My name is Naomi, and I live in a world where hope is outlawed"*, and then the screen dips to black. When it comes back, there's a closeup of her putting on a glove. Then another of her tying her boots. Then another of her slipping a mask over her hair. You never see her face. The music builds. The narration continues, and finally ends with a badass proclamation, like, *"but at night, I become something else entirely"*. Then we see a silhouette of our superhero in her superhero costume. But before we actually see the person, we cut to the book cover! *Boom! Exploding drums! Fog horn! Pre-order your copy today!*

You have just been teased without seeing anything that would ruin your ability to imagine the characters, or the settings, or the plot.

This style works with objects, too. Flashing images of items important to the plot or symbolic in some way is a very effective way to tease your audience. Leave them wanting to know more. Make them *need* to click that 'buy book' button.

The teaser can be done with text, photos, footage, music, even just colored screens if you're creative enough. And it keeps your trailer's timer down to clickable size, because people are much likelier to watch a short video than a long one.

Graphics/Text/Animation Video

This is for authors who may not be able to capture video or photographs of actors, or those stories with a more abstract subject matter. Graphics are an extremely powerful tool, and we've all seen some excellent all-graphics trailers or commercials.

Using animated icons, symbols, logos, and text keeps the viewer's eyes moving, and can help drive home a complicated message.

One popular style of text-only video is known as "kinetic typography", which essentially means "text that moves". This is typically timed out with some sort of narration, the words appearing as the narrator speaks them, but it doesn't have to be.

That style has been around for a while now, so if you're going for kinetic typography, you might want to find a way to make it stylistically yours by adding icons, animations, or really punchy narration. A quick internet search will churn up hundreds of these types of videos, so do a little homework before diving in.

You can also create a sense of setting by using graphics or shapes that work as symbols for your story. A tree icon can work just as well as a shot of a tree. You can even use abstract shapes to help tell a story. Imagine combining text with a heart monitor line. Maybe a bit outdated, but you get the gist of what I'm saying.

Be warned, however, that graphics-only pieces can very quickly slip into looking cheesy or tacky if not done by someone with an artistic eye. Be sure you (or your animator) have a really good sense of visual design.

Graphics also include any type of animations, cartoons, or 'flying text' that you sometimes see in epic movie trailers. Currently, text has taken the place of film trailer narrators, and there's no reason it shouldn't be just as effective with book trailers. I mean, words are kind of an author's thing, right?

> **PRO TIP**: *If you have favorable reviews, animated text is a great way to highlight that.*

Critic's Testimonial Video

Think of a documentary. The story is mainly told through on-screen testimonials, and a testimonial book video works in just the same way. A critic's testimonial video features critics, experts, or clients speaking onscreen about the purpose of the book, the topics it covers, or even about how wonderful the book itself is.

This style can also be combined with other images (which I refer to as 'b-roll'), music, text, or a litany of other stylistic additions to create what amounts to a marketing documentary video, or commercial, that has the feeling of authenticity. If you've got people who are willing to say excellent things about your book or your book's topic, then use them!

In a similar way, infomercials use this technique a lot when they cut to the 'expert' or 'doctor' testimonials.

The point of critic, client, or expert testimonials is to establish the credibility of your book. It is also an effective way to frame a problem or discuss a solution. And we see this style *all the time* on scientific TV, discovery, history, or educational shows, reality TV, in the movies, commercials, and even print advertising.

If you've never filmed an on-screen interview before, have no fear. I provide tips and tricks later that will help you get the most out of your testimonials.

Author's Testimonial Video

There may be very good reasons for you, the author, to speak about your own book. Especially if you're ridiculously good-looking...

Okay, I'm kidding, but not entirely. I've heard rumors of authors and celebrities getting their big breaks simply because they were easy on the eyes. Humans trust and enjoy good-looking people.

Aside from your physical assets, you, as the author, probably have a compelling story about why the book was written, or may be making an argument to readers as to why the book is so important to read. You may be an expert in a particular field and thus the most qualified person to talk about the subject matter.

This approach may work well if you're querying an agent and want a way to digitally introduce yourself, show that agent you're a knowledgeable, personable, and saavy marketer of your own book. You don't need to make a dramatic trailer because the book may be edited and changed by the time the agents and editors and publishers finish with it, but that shouldn't stop you from telling your *personal* story to the agent.

There is an author I know who has written over 17 gritty crime novels. He only got into writing because he was in jail for many of the crimes he wrote about, and the act of writing actually became part of his rehabilitation. That's the kind of story that's just begging for an author's testimonial, because readers are more likely to pick up his books if they know the story behind why they were written. An agent is more likely to want to read the manuscript if she hears his story. It also goes towards improving his credibility as a crime writer (his novels are fictional, though, so many of the details have been fudged...so he tells me).

The point is, there may be a very good reason to put yourself in front of the camera. You're the one most likely to make a compelling argument for your own book.

The "Explainer" Video

Sometimes you want a video that isn't so...artsy. Perhaps your content doesn't lend itself to dramatic scenarios. Perhaps you think trailers are cheesy. Perhaps you're sick of exploding drums. Whatever the reason, there are millions of ways to advertise for your book without making a 'movie trailer'.

This is a style I call the "Explainer Video" because it is still going to get audiences interested in the story, but it doesn't require acting out scenarios. Using video, photographs, cartoons, or even hand-drawings along with narration and music, you can show the setting, background, conflict, and character of your story in a straightforward manner without having anyone pretend to be your characters. This *explains* your story, rather than trying to pull you in through a dramatic recreation.

Since a book video is essentially a commercial for your book, it's best to think of all of the different types of commercials you've seen. They don't all involve a "story" to tell you what the product is. Sometimes they just show you what the product is and why it's so great. They tell you what you can expect when you get that product. An explainer video essentially does this for your book.

Be aware, however, you're at risk of breaking the age-old rule *show don't tell*, because it's way too easy to over-explain a story. Make sure your explanation is riveting, well-written, and compelling.

Everything Else

It would be impossible to outline every type of video or style you could choose because the possibilities are endless. By the time you read this, there may be new popular styles or ways of telling stories that I didn't even think of. Maybe 3D will be popular again, or 360-degree video, maybe smell-o-vision will be invented, maybe interactive commercials will be all the rage (I'm dubious about this), but if you're truly new to the idea of creating video or marketing for your book, it helps to know what some of the main options are. I encourage you to find ways to combine, stretch, change, or completely reinvent the different ways of making audiences aware of your book.

Although there are drastically different approaches to making a book trailer, the techniques remain the same. No matter the medium, good visual storytelling is composed of some universal base elements. Let's examine those elements.

NUTS & BOLTS & TRAILER HITCHES: HOW TO CREATE YOUR BOOK TRAILER

The creation of pretty much any type of visual media very loosely follows the same path from concept through completion. This outline is a time-tested process that makes film, video, television, radio, and multimedia projects just a little bit easier to access and much more organized. I've seen many, many projects go down in flames simply because those in charge tried to skip these steps or cut corners. I've also seen a few doomed projects turn out quite successfully because the creators took the time to plot out their journey properly. Planning is important.

In it's most basic form, the secret sauce to production is made up of the following ingredients:

- **Scripting**
- **Pre-production**
- **Production**
- **Post-production**
- **Distribution**

It's that simple. If you aren't sure what I mean by each of these steps just yet, that's okay. From here on out we will be focusing on each one and how to accomplish it. I will even sprinkle in a few pro tips and point out a few obstacles to avoid along the way.

Scripting: Finding the Magic

The first thing you'll want to do when creating your book video is to write a script for it. This doesn't have to be an Oscar-worthy piece of film history. It's a place to start turning your ideas into concrete goals, a way to organize your thoughts. The script is a blueprint for what you'll be making, in the same way you likely started with an outline for the book you've written.

Not everyone starts with a script, as some people start with a song or an image, and that's okay, too. By "scripting" I really mean finding a tangible way to organize your thoughts and inspiration into a plan. If you can listen to a certain piece of music and "see it all come together," then you should follow your own muse. For most people, however, writing out what should appear on screen is the most important step in taking your book trailer from concept to completion.

Your script is the backbone of any video project, and without one there's really nothing to make a video *about*. But how do you boil down your 100,000-word novel into a two-minute script? How will you even know it's two minutes long? How do you write something that happens on screen at the same time something is being said?

These are all vital questions, but they're not the most important question. In order to start writing your trailer, you need to address your main conundrum: **what is your story about?**

Seems simple, right? If you think so, try writing it down. Right now. In one sentence. Authors who have been writing query letters for a while or who have been practicing their elevator pitches may be able to do this on the spot. Most of us, however, will have to take some time to boil down the roots of our books in order to simply explain what it is the book is about.

> **PRO TIP**: *We often struggle with succinctly explaining what our story is about, and sometimes it comes out too long or boring or cliché. Instead, ask yourself* **who** *the story is about. For example, take the movie Jurassic Park.* <u>What</u> *is the movie about? It's about dinosaurs that escape from a modern theme park and attack the guests.* <u>Who</u> *is the movie about? It's about Dr. Alan Grant struggling to save two children from certain death when dinosaurs escape from a theme park. It's a subtle difference, but explaining who your story is about helps personalize it, thus making it more engaging. People like stories about people.*

For the sake of your script, you don't need a Shakespearean soliloquy, so stop sweating. You just need a good grasp of what it is you'd like to get across to your audience, because that's what you'll build your script around. And remember your video can be different in style than your actual book, because it doesn't appear anywhere in the book! So try to break away from the idea that your video should be a reenactment of a scene from your novel.

Instead, start with answers to the following questions. You might recognize them from earlier.

For fiction:

1. Who is the main character?

2. What does he/she want?

3. What is standing in the way?

And for nonfiction:

1. What problem exists?

2. What or how does this book propose to solve/treat this problem?

3. Why is this book different than other books of the same kind?

4. What are the author's credentials?

Although the script for the trailer does not actually appear anywhere in the book, it is designed to get the important information—and emotions—across in a short time. Perhaps there is a block of narration that your main protagonist (or antagonist!) says that is both telling of your story and engaging to an audience. A serial killer saying something creepy about his next victim. A young orphan girl on her own describing how she's found joy in the darkest parts of this old, dirty city. An alien telling us that it comes in peace. Something like that can work as the narration, or at least a sound bite.

Perhaps you'd rather turn your main plot points into on-screen text that appears along with loud musical bangs. You see the shot of a girl in the rain, then cut to words on screen saying "One girl, alone in the world", then cut to a bloody knife and back to words that read, "will find her revenge". You get the idea.

Or perhaps you'd like to have your nonfiction experts explain the problem your book addresses through on-screen testimonials. You'll have to write out the questions you want them to answer.

There are millions of options, but the important part is you've started to answer those three or four questions. They really are the ingredients to anything gripping and engaging. You'll also start to notice that by answering these questions and thinking in this way, you've already started developing an idea. Hopefully you're starting to think of things you'd like to show off in the trailer, and you're starting to see pictures in your mind's eye.

As you continue to develop your script, don't forget that mind's eye. Many authors struggle with the idea of putting something interesting on the screen because *they think like authors*. In other words, they think in words. But remember that video is a *visual* medium, and pictures accomplish more in this world. Don't fall into the trap of imagining your video as a piece of writing and never think about what you will *see* when watching it. This means writing in terms of settings and action scenes, in a way. It's great to have a really engaging narrator speaking—and it works really well in a *book*—but as your narrator is speaking, what will the audience be seeing on the screen? A black screen? That's not very exciting. You can do much, much better.

Writing a script is also a bit of a writing exercise. It's a great challenge to try to write something that will be persuasive and engaging, and is *about* your book. When crafting this message and imagining what you want to appear on screen and how you want to tell your story, there is one other very important goal to take into consideration: the **Call To Action**. *What do you want your audience to do?*

This is neither figurative nor abstract. Ask yourself, when a person watches this video, *what* do you want that person to *do* once they've finished? Do you want them to click on a link to buy the book? Do you want them to go to a website and find out more about your cause? Do you want them to put a note on their calendar about the date of the book release? This little detail is so very important because it answers that unspoken question the audience asks itself, namely, *"what do I do now?"*

A CTA also gives you, dear writer, a focus when crafting your message. It can even give you a look at which type of format would help best achieve this goal.

For example, if you want the audience to visit a website and learn more about a cause, then somewhere in your video you'll want to explain a little bit about that cause and what a person can accomplish by going to said website. That may also influence your stylistic decisions, maybe pushing you towards a testimonial-with-experts-style video, rather than a dramatic recreation.

We'll dive into CTAs more in a later chapter, but for now, don't forget that call to action when building your script. It's how you'll end your script, 99% of the time.

Script Formats

Okay, so you've got your overview now. You have a rough idea of what you'd like the trailer to be about, and what type of trailer you'd like to make. Time to get down to the nuts and bolts of writing this sucker, and that includes the script format. Just as there are different styles of books, there are different styles and formats for scripts. Following these formats (or your own rough approximation) will help you line up the visuals with the audio, and will also help you get an idea of the timing, pace, style, and even the look of your trailer. Although there are dozens of scriptwriting formats, you really only need to choose between two of them, unless you're working with a large team.

The key to any scriptwriting format is easy communication. Someone who knows nothing about you or your writing style should be able to pick up a script and know what the video will look like and approximately how long it will be. To that end, if you're writing a script that only you will be working from, you don't have to be a stickler with the formatting. Whatever is easiest for you to understand is what you should go with. The same goes for working with a team. If there is a format that everyone helping you can easily understand, go for it. Typically, however, one of the two following formats tends to be clearest, and the most helpful for those new to scripting. Which style you prefer is a personal choice, so go with what's comfortable.

These two styles are the *traditional screenplay* and the *AV-style script*. You'll note that what most people associate as a stage play is NOT common practice for a video. Most professionals cringe when someone writes a "script" in the style they remember from reading plays in high school. This isn't just a snobby disinclination towards works of the stage, but rather a functional decision. The 'stage performance' style of script doesn't easily communicate the things you will see on the screen, or the timing.

Traditional Screenplay

The first, and most common, script format you're likely to see and use is the **traditional screenplay**. This format is used from Hollywood to your hometown for just about any professional or semi-professional dramatic production, and is commonly referred to as the default "script format". Television shows, movies, student films, and all the projects in between are (supposed to be) written in screenplay format. There are lots of rules and formatting nuances you can easily get lost in, but for your purposes you really only need to worry about three main aspects.

1. Scene Heading/Description
    a. This is a line at the top of each scene that tells the reader—very quickly—what the scene is, the interior or exterior location, and the time of day. It typically looks something like this: **SCENE 1: INT. JANE'S HOUSE – DAY**

2. Action, Description, and Camera Direction
    a. Below that heading is typically a description or line of action, written in present tense and lower-case, giving the reader more details about what is happening on screen. *Remember* that you are writing for a screen, so unlike a novel, this is supposed to be bare-bones and only concerns what the audience can see or hear. No flowery language, no smells or feelings in the air, nothing that isn't visible. Just something as simple as, "Mike hits John in the face. John falls to the floor and grabs the gun. He points the gun at Mike, who raises his hands in surrender." Keep it simple.
    b. Throughout the script you will also need to explain what the audience will see, and anything you can't get through in the dialogue. In order to accomplish that, just add a paragraph of action or description.
    c. Within the action you can also describe camera moves and suggested camera angles. If you're writing for a major Hollywood movie, this is frowned upon (the director will choose the camera angles, thank you very much), but if you're writing for your own purposes, it does help to throw in a little "camera moves in closer to the gun" camera direction.

3. Dialogue/Narration
    a. What good is all of the action and description without some cheeky dialogue? Dialogue is just about anything a character or narrator will say. This is separated from both the action and descriptions by a heading with the character's name, and below that the words they're saying. It is usually centered and justified so as to stand out.

Here's a brief example of what a script format looks like. Take note of where the description, action, camera direction, and dialogue goes. Again, this format exists for clarity and ease of reading, so if you break a few of the rules it's not a big deal so long as you are clearly communicating what you want.

INT. KITCHEN - NIGHT

The kitchen is dark, light streaming in only from the streetlights outside and a few blinking electric sparks. There's a faint hint of smoke in the air, and the microwave has a cracked face. The counters are littered with broken electronics.

KYLE, SARA, and BILL stand together in the door, staring into the kitchen. Kyle sniffs the air.

> KYLE:
> Smells like you tried to microwave a skunk.

SARA runs over to the counter, ignoring Kyle and picking up the broken electronics. She points towards the refrigerator without looking back.

> SARA:
> The beer is over there. Now shut up and let the grownups work. We've got to figure out what went wrong with the flux capacitor.

Kyle cracks open a beer while BILL walks over next to Sara to inspect the damage. Behind them, Kyle takes a sip of beer and belches. He glances around the kitchen, taking stock. The camera follows his gaze, looking out the back window.

> KYLE:
> You know, I am a person. I have feelings. When you insult me, I hurt. When you cut me, I bleed. When you—hey, what was that?

> BILL (distracted)
> Hmm...? What was what?

> KYLE:
> There in the back—there it goes again!

He points through the back window into the yard, where there appears to be a trick-or-treater's mask hanging from a tree. With a loud CRACK, the window shatters.

CUT TO BLACK

As you can see, it's easy to paint a picture very quickly, and there's really no reason for excessively verbose diction, if you catch my drift. Script format is all about clarity. It's also a quick way to size up the length of a finished project, because if formatted properly, one page of script is equal to one minute of screen time. Pretty clever, huh? But that also gives you an idea if you've never scripted anything before: two pages is two minutes. You'll be surprised how much practice it takes to keep your ideas contained within two pages.

If you'd like to learn more about screenplay format, there are resources galore, some of them free and some of them costly. There are books upon books about both formatting and writing for the screen, if you're thinking of making the switch to screenwriting. There are programs that do the formatting for you, templates to follow, and even interactive ways to share scripts. There are always bigger and better and smarter programs available, and I encourage you to find the resources you are most comfortable with.

Audio/Visual Script

The **AV Style Script** format, also known as **Audio/Visual**, Left/Right, or even Column Script format, is another option that's extremely popular with video productions. In particular, the AV format is seen in commercials, corporate videos, and pretty much anything non-Hollywood where the scriptwriter may be sharing their work with those who are *not* familiar with the film industry.

For most uses, and for most self-publishing authors, this format is the easiest to understand and the most useful. It simultaneously shows what will be on screen and what the audience will be hearing. It is designed to be instantly understandable without the need for descriptions, scene headings, and other screenplay-style formatting requirements. It's also easy enough to make on any word processor, so there isn't a software obstacle.

The AV format is essentially a table with two columns; one for the audio and one for the visuals. That table can be broken up into blocks, much like a spreadsheet, which indicate scene changes, paragraph changes, or any change in visual, style, or tone. Where and how you divide your AV script is a personal preference, so simply divide it in a way that is easiest to understand. I typically divide my AV scripts by creating a new block for each complete thought.

Since I firmly believe in the adage "show, don't tell", below you'll see an example of an AV script.

AUDIO	VISUAL
Music rises as the scene opens. **NARRATOR**: "In a world where reading is outlawed."	Fade from black. The video opens on a sunrise over a futuristic city.
NARRATOR: "One outlaw…" *Sound effects of birds flying overhead.*	We see the closeup of a cowboy hat. Then a wider shot of a rough cowboy standing in the middle of the city. In his hand is a book.

NARRATOR: "...will dare to read between the lines."	A book on a table catches fire and the pages burn in slow motion.
NARRATOR: "From the bestselling author of 'The Deaf Musician' comes a tale of heroism in a time of fear."	The camera follows the smoke from the book up towards the sky, where we see the silhouette of the cowboy in the background.
Music rises, and a whoosh sound effect hits as the graphic flies in.	**GRAPHIC TEXT**: *Black text on a paper-texture background with the quote typing on:* *"One of the best books about reading I've ever read." – E-publisher's press*
NARRATOR: "Richard Bailey's 'The Blind Reader'."	The book graphic from above then slams shut, revealing the cover, THE BLIND READER. The book itself sits on a white background.
NARRATOR: "Available wherever books are sold." *Music rises then fades out.*	As the book fades to white, black text appears with the contact information and a link to the Amazon sales page. Fade to black.

As you can see, this format makes it easy to see what each shot will look like, when certain lines will be said, and any sounds, graphics or text that will appear. A casual reader should be able to figure out what's going on in each frame without seeing a storyboard (more on that in the preproduction chapter).

Which script format you ultimately choose is merely the mechanical aspect of scripting your video. Let's go a little deeper into the fun part; actually *writing* the thing.

Writing the Script

When I create book videos—or any videos for that matter—I spend a good deal of time writing the script and imagining what each image will be, how the cameras will move, what the graphics will look like, and even the music that will go with it. It's a chance to make a completely new project that is in some ways independent of the book. It's an interesting challenge. I encourage you to see your video in the same light, not as just some condensed version of your book, but as a strong piece of writing in its own right. This makes the challenge and the process fun—it gives you a chance to stretch your writerly wings and look at your story from a different angle.

You get to write, and imagine, and pontificate. A good video—actually a good *anything*—always begins with solid writing. Take the time to get it right. Once you've written and re-written and revised and tweaked and twerked the final version for the umpteenth time, you should end up knowing exactly what you want the trailer to sound like and to look like, start-to-finish, second-to-second.

Every video is different, but most book videos can start in the same place. If you're wondering where the starting line is, luckily there is a really easy way to research your field: watch movie trailers! Seriously, you can learn so much by watching the similarities you see throughout movie trailers that you enjoy. Generally the public prefers something that is familiar yet unique and engaging, and what that is changes with the times. By watching the most recent movie trailers and analyzing which aspects keep you glued to the screen and which techniques help the trailer achieve its goal, you'll start to learn a bit about the culture and style of your viewers.

At the time of this original version (2015), for example, text flying on screen with loud foghorn noises was a popular way to get across any necessary 'narration'. This style has replaced the traditional, grovelly-voiced narrator who starts by announcing, "In a world where…". While revising this in 2020, the current trend is "popular music played in as a slow, dramatic cover," and by the time you read this, there may be new techniques and styles, and the "dramatic music" may be just as passé as the "Inception Foghorn." It's always changing. Typically, however, you can't go wrong by following some simple rules.

Just like the finished book itself, every video should have a story. That means a beginning, middle, and end. Or, to be more descriptive, a **hook**, a **rising action**, and a **conclusion** (*hook, build, and boom* if you like). This doesn't have to be interpreted literally, but every good trailer has these elements at the very least on an emotional level.

For instance, let's imagine a horror film trailer. It starts off with a creepy voice whispering through the phone. On screen you see a shot of a dark doorway creeping open by itself, almost inviting you in (**hook**). You then see various shots of the main character, shots that help set up the tension by revealing a little bit about the plot of the story through her dialogue and actions, and also revealing the conflict. In this example maybe we cut to a few quick shots that establish that there was a lab accident, creating…something. Maybe we see quick cuts of something getting loose. A tail here. A claw there. The main character frantically turns to her lab partner, insisting that they've broken the laws of nature. We then see a few shots of the creature's victims, wrapped in a nasty, bodily goo. The shadow of some unknown creature is cast across a wall, morphing and changing as the tense music builds. All of this serves as the **rising action** (**build**).

While this is going on, the audience is learning key points about the conflict. They know it's a creature feature. They know it escaped from the lab and is killing people. They know the main character is likely responsible for catching the creature—or at least surviving the night. There's all sorts of good information we can work into this section, because the rising action is the longest part of the commercial. It's also the 'information dump'. It's the part of the trailer where the setting, theme, style, and plot points are established and fleshed out a little bit. The rising action is the meat of the trailer, and it's the most difficult part to make interesting. Just like writing your query letter, you're going to be tempted to throw a *lot* of information into the rising action section. But it's always more effective to keep it simple, sharp, and moving. The audience only needs the absolute bare minimum of information. You want to establish the world and then tease the audience, nothing more.

> **PRO TIP**: *There is a very fine line to walk between giving away too much information and failing to provide enough context— thus confusing the audience. Always have someone unfamiliar with the story look over your script to make sure they understand what your book is about. And if they say they don't, actually listen to them. You won't be there to explain the story to each viewer, so the trailer must do it for you.*

Finally, we come to our **conclusion**. In this example, it's our hero gripping the phone in horror as the voice on the other end of the phone says, "It's no longer in the lab. It's in your house." The creature leaps from the closet, then **BOOM!** Title, CTA, the end. You can change this up by having an additional post-boom hook after the title comes up. Most horror trailers do this now, giving you one last scare before you go.

And it's not just horror trailers. Take a look at action trailers, or even comedies and romances. There is always some type of hook or introduction ("In a world where…"), followed by explanation and world-building. For an action or adventure story, the rising action would be explaining the main goal of the journey and the obstacles characters will face. A comedy may set up the situation and give away a few jokes during the rising action.

In almost every case, the conclusion leaves the audience with an unanswered question, whether overt or implied. This leaves viewers with the feeling that they need to find out what is going to happen next…hopefully giving them enough incentive to go out and purchase the book *right now* because they simply *must know.* A final joke for a comedy, introduction of a new, larger, unexplained obstacle for an action movie, a hint that the creature is stronger than we ever imagined in a horror movie. This wraps up the book trailer and opens up the chance for you to show off the cover, CTA, and purchasing information.

These rules and formulae are not set in stone. If you come up with a creative idea that has nothing to do with this formula, it may work really, really well. The beautiful thing about writing is that we are always imagining and innovating news ways to tell stories, and writing your book video is no different.

Before you get too far with your trusty quill of imagination, however, a word of warning: even the best-written video can suffer catastrophically if not planned properly. So before you get too excited, consider a few tips when writing.

Write Something You Can Actually Shoot

Reality check time. Writers (especially fiction writers) like to create beautiful, imaginative worlds, and thus want to show them off. Be careful with this when writing your script, because it's vitally important that you be real with yourself. Make sure your script is feasible. You may have an epic Viking vs. alien battle as the centerpiece for the book, but it's unlikely you have the resources to pull together 1,000 extras decked out in full-on Viking war costumes that will clash with 1,000 extras in convincing alien costumes. By no means limit yourself creatively, but keep perspective in mind. Authenticity and quality are huge deals, so be sure what you write you can actually pull off. Even if it's only one alien and one Viking, be sure you have access to convincing costumes. The same goes for action sequences, romantic sequences, and things that require lots of money. No one wants to see a really poorly-executed stunt or a clearly fake fist fight.

Creating a convincing world is particularly tricky with period pieces (past or future). Your friends are unlikely to have 1920's garb lying around, for instance. Instead of seeing a limited resource as an obstacle, though, think of it as a creative exercise: how can you advertise your intense story without breaking your budget? I can't give you the answer, but the script is the best place to go searching for it.

Maybe showing close-up shots of important items from the book may help build the drama without costing you much. In fact, I did this with one of my own book trailers: rather than show off a violent murder, a large crime scene, and other important scenes from the book, I used a dramatic close-up of a bloody knife followed by a strip of crime scene tape fluttering in the rain, then a rose crushed in the mud. This created a sense of mystery and intrigue without giving away anything important in the book. Those types of tricks are a visual version of every writer's friend—symbolism.

Be sure you've written something that your actors/filmmakers/crew can actually pull off. And I'm not talking just about special effects and lots of extras. If you don't have access to Actor's Guild-level talent, you may want to omit that emotional crying monologue. Directing, acting, and camera work are as important to pulling off a successful video as any other part of it. Many people take acting and directing for granted only to find out how incredibly difficult it really is. Don't be one of those people—know your limits and your strengths, and make sure your script works to your strengths.

Timing is Everything

Make sure your script is short. Even if your book is very, very long and involved, online viewers' attention spans are not. Even theatrical trailers with millions of dollars don't usually go over three minutes. I recommend keeping your book video between 15 seconds and two minutes. Remember that online viewers are more likely to click and watch something that is *short*. Some commercials are as short as three seconds.

In order to keep it short, a good place to start is with your query letter, or your "elevator pitch", if you have one. Don't know what an elevator pitch is? Imagine you're visiting an agency in New York, and you happen to get into the elevator with an agent. You've got until the agent gets off that elevator to explain your book, why it is special, and what makes it worth purchasing. A script that does the same can go a long way.

Make it Idiot-Proof

Make sure your video clearly explains what the book is and where someone can find it. Make sure that CTA is crystal clear and idiot-proof. In fact, make sure you consider whether your trailer makes it clear that you're advertising for a *book*. Sure, *you* know it's a book, but what's clear to you may not be so clear to an unacquainted audience member. A random scene with your book cover slapped on the end isn't going to get much attention because it's confusing. No one knows what it's about or where to get it!

Context is so important within the video, too. Actors doing random "things" or yelling random one-liners with music playing loudly does not make a good trailer. It's confusing. It's also important that someone can watch the video and know at least a little bit about what the book is *about.* Otherwise, you've wasted your time and your viewer's.

I see this all the time, and can't help but wonder what the authors were thinking. Viewers want to know the facts, quickly, and if they get to the end of your video and *must buy your book*, you want to make sure they clearly know where to go. This includes a link to your sales page, email list, website, or other place someone can purchase your masterpiece.

Head in the Clouds, Feet on the Ground

Be realistic with your expectations. This goes hand-in-hand with writing something that is feasible to pull off. Remember that every video production has its own unique problems, and the more you can prepare yourself and know what to expect, the better off you'll be. This also requires coming to terms with the idea that your video may not be popular right off the bat. There's no way to *force* something to go viral. Just like publishing a book, managing your expectations for how many people will see your video, and how many of those will actually buy the book, is vital to remaining sane. Posting one link on Facebook will not guarantee 1,000,000 views. You have to work at it.

Write for your Wallet

Keep your budget in mind. Everything has a cost, and if you've written in lots of effects, crazy sets, and expensive props, you may end up paying more for your video than you can reasonably expect to make from your book! Have a general idea of what things cost, what you can get for free, and which strings you can pull to get people to help you.

Perform it Yourself

Read it out loud. Make sure it flows. Make sure it's as short as you think it is. Reading your script aloud is a time-honored tradition when it comes to commercial timing. It also helps you hear lines that may sound good on paper but fall flat when spoken, and it helps you know when you've said something right or wrong. Especially if you're reading to a trusted accomplice, notice the parts that make you embarrassed to read. Chances are, if you find yourself apologizing for a part or blushing over something in the script, it doesn't belong.

Another trick is to pick a music track that you think would work with it, and try to write to that. Follow the ups and downs of the track.

Write It like You Stole It

If you're looking for guidance or inspiration, turn to work that already exists. You can even copy a current movie trailer or commercial, and repurpose the idea for yourself—don't copy directly, but that's hardly a concern if you're trying to mimic a million-dollar movie. Since trailers tend to have a base formula, copying that formula and repurposing it for your work is a smart move.

Scripting the Unscripted

Finally, you may be wondering what to do if you're planning to use testimonials for your non-fiction book. How do you script for that? Well, there are two ways. First and most obvious is to actually write exactly what you want your subjects to say. This has the advantage of saving time on set and allowing you more control over exactly what is said. However, this approach usually backfires.

Most interview subjects don't or can't convincingly say what you'd like them to. It's not their fault, if they *could* act, they'd probably get paid to do that instead of whatever it is they're an expert of. This happens a lot when non-actors get in front of a camera and have to try to recite from memory. It can come across like a bad children's play where small children haltingly read from the Declaration of Independence, stumbling through it and sweating through their shirts from the embarrassment. It also lacks authenticity and spontaneity.

The second option is to leave spots in the script with the subject of that sound bite. You're making a note in the script where you'd like someone to talk about a certain topic, but you're not writing *ver batim* what you expect them to say. Rather, you're making a note that, in that spot, someone should say something "along the lines of" *x*. They should "talk about" *x, y,* and *z*. This leaves it open to the interview subject to say what they feel in their own words. This typically comes off as genuine. If you really want to challenge yourself, ask your subject a series of questions and try to cut together a fully-formed story in the edit. This is typically how documentaries are made, though it is a bit more time-consuming and comes with its own set of challenges.

Finally—and I say this sincerely—enjoy the exercise. It's going to be miserable if you don't find some sort of redeeming factor in this process. Write something that you want to see because you think it would be interesting! Try something new, or something exciting, something that makes you enthusiastic about the project.

Pre-Production: Where the Magic Actually Happens

We as writers get the joy of expressing ourselves on paper. You know, where you're safe and the word processor can't disagree with you. This joy, however, is often intimately entwined with deep trepidation because, well, you have to *show your work to other people.* The same is true for your script you'd like to turn into a video—in fact, it's harder because your work isn't finished yet. It can be quite difficult—and potentially embarrassing—to share your creative vision with others, especially when in its naked early form. But this is what preproduction is all about. You've got your script, now you need to develop the plan that will take you from the page to the screen. Preproduction is every bit of planning, vision, and yes, work that goes into a video production before you actually shoot. This includes creating a budget, finding a location, building a shooting schedule, finding a crew and a camera, casting actors, imagining costumes, locating props, and in general tending to every single detail. It is said that a movie is made in preproduction, the rest is just painting by numbers.

Most people have never even heard of this process because it's neither glamorous nor exciting (for some reason logistics and planning seem to have a certain lack of sex appeal). I don't care. I don't care that it seems boring. Or difficult. Or you think you can just 'wing it'. You will fail if you don't at least put some forethought into your production. Preproduction is the absolute most important stage of any production, where the rubber meets the road, where the bacon meets the Teflon. More important than the production day, more important than the editing, more important than the script, preproduction is all about making a plan and sticking to it. It is important. Do it.

Now that I've scared you into submission, allow me to explain what exactly it is you'll be doing in preproduction. I'll preface this by saying, again, that every production is different so some of these steps don't apply:

• Sharing Your Idea

- Storyboarding/Pre-Viz
- Budgeting
- Location Scouting
- Scheduling
- Locating Crew
- Locating Cast/Interview Subjects
- Final Prep

Getting Started and Sharing Your Idea

Sharing your idea and asking people to help you make it is by far the hardest part of pre-production. Especially if you're not totally sure if people will understand your script without seeing it. Have faith in yourself. If it works in your head, if you can read your script and see your vision, then trust that you'll be able to communicate that vision to others. This isn't an easy skill, and it takes time to truly develop it, but I know you can do it. Open up your writer's room door and tell a few people about your idea. See what they say. Test it out with close friends and significant others to make sure they understand it.

You may think I'm trying to hand-hold the weak-hearted and put their fears at ease, and you can skip this step if you're sure of yourself and your work. If you believe that, then you, my friend, need to take a step back and *definitely* share your work with others before going any further. Getting perspective on our ideas is vitally important, and it helps you hunt out problems and issues early on that you can address or change before you've wasted any time or money.

It is important to be sure you can clearly explain your script and what you'll need to complete it because everyone else will be looking to you when they have questions about how it should look/feel/sound/etc. Make sure you're prepared by sharing with others at an early stage. They may help guide your story in the right direction.

Storyboarding and Previsualization

Remember how I urged you to think very hard about what the audience will *see* when they watch the video? It's time to do that again. The best way to ensure you, your crew, and eventually your audience are all on the same page is to have a visual representation of the finished product. This is called a storyboard. Well, sometimes it's an animatic. Or a picture board. Or a scratch track. Or a look board. There are lots of different terms, but overall you take my point. Most videos need some sort of previsualization, even if it isn't a full-blown, shot-by-shot Hollywood storyboard.

Perhaps you only need to write out different text boxes that will appear. Perhaps you were able to find an example somewhere online that's a perfect match for what you're doing. Perhaps you just need to scribble notes on the side of your script. Whatever your process, you need to somehow determine exactly what each shot will look like, and communicate that in a *visual* way. This helps you express your vision clearly to anyone else involved in the process, and it helps you continue to wrap your mind around the idea that people will *see* this, not read it.

It is very important for writers to deeply understand this concept—that video is inherently different from writing. I cannot overstate this. Storyboarding is important for everyone, but it is especially important for writers because we are so used to communicating through words that people read. That means readers create their own images in their heads. In a video, you're creating the images for them. And it's easy to forget that. So don't. Draw it up. Make *sure* you'll show your audience the images you see in your head when you read your script. Please, oh, please.

How do you make a storyboard, then? It's really easy, actually.

Take your script, which most likely is in AV style, and replace the visual column with an image. Either draw it or find a picture online to represent it. More or less, you're done. Or at least, you could be. I suggest you make things easier on yourself, though, and do more work now so you have to do less work later.

When storyboarding, remember that each line of text can be represented by several different images, and each scene may include several different camera angles. You'll want a drawn image for each camera angle. Every time the camera moves, you should have a new image on your storyboard. For instance, if you have a conversation between John and Jayne, you will probably need at least two camera angles: a shot of John, and a shot of Jayne. If it's a longer scene, you probably need a wide shot as well, and if they indicate something such as an object they're holding, then you probably need a shot of that object. Try to think about each and every second of your script. What will people see?

If you'd like to take it even further, you can create a moving storyboard or an animatic. This involves recording a 'scratch track' of the audio and laying images over it in your editing timeline. Essentially it's like a stick-figure version of your video in real time. Let me clarify further.

Pretend you have a narrator for your video. You don't have that narrator yet, but most of you probably have a voice of your own, correct? Record yourself narrating, and playing each character. Even if there are different characters talking, you can still mimic them (don't worry, you won't ever have to share your annoying false falsetto with anyone). This stand-in recording is known as a scratch track. The goal is to get an idea of the timing for your video, and when each image will appear, when each cut will happen. You can record your voice with most computers or tablets nowadays, or even on your phone.

Lay this scratch track into your editing program (more on that later) and scan your storyboard drawings in. Then, lay those images in time with the scratch track you've recorded. You can even add in music or text effects to this. The idea is to have a 'rough draft' of the video, from start to finish, *before you start making it*. This will help you decide if you need more shots, or fewer shots, or if your narration is too long or too short, and in general will help you visualize the finished product and work out any creative kinks. Use your imagination, and you'll start to see your video come to life. If you're not too embarrassed, you can even show this to others to communicate your ideas more clearly.

I'm sure there are ideas out there that would not benefit from some sort of storyboard, but I can't think what they would be. No matter what type of video you're creating, you should have some sort of visual plan as to what it will look like. Even if it's as simple as finding an example video online and saying, "it will look like that". You might not get all the details right (most likely your actor won't look like a stick figure and your location will be more than a box), but you should at least have *an idea* of what you want before moving on. This stage is to help you with that idea.

Budgeting

Ah, the money part. We all love making it, we all hate spending it. Sadly, it is a fact of life that there are costs of some type associated with using any resource. Those costs are not always monetary, but can usually be accounted for in some way or another. When putting together the plan for your video, taking all of those costs into account and being aware of them is a vital part of creating a successful project without losing your shirt.

There is a stigma that budgeting is difficult, and the mere mention of creating a budget makes many people decide they don't have the money to do...well, anything. And so they either skip this step or completely give up out of the fear of doing something wrong. But if you think about it, you create budgets all the time! Think of your production budget as a recipe for the parts of your video, or as a shopping list. For the most part, you're simply writing down what you need and how much each of those things will cost. It *can* get more complicated than that, but it doesn't have to.

You still don't believe me? Okay, fine. Let's dive into the details of a typical video budget, what you'll need, and how to do it without spending any money. Be aware that while you can do something for a zero budget, there is always some sort of cost for the resources you use, whether it be money, time, services, or a Godfather-style, *when I ask you for a favor in the future...*

The most accessible form of budget—and most likely the most useful for your needs—is going to be a **line item budget**. Essentially, this is a list of the resources you'll need—the line items—and the costs associated with those. It is important to be as inclusive and specific with your line items as possible, even if they cost you absolutely nothing. This way you can use your budget as a checklist of things you need. It's as much of an organization strategy as it is an accounting tool.

For the sake of this example, let's assume you're going to make a dramatic book trailer that you've written to include a narrator, some graphic text, and two scenes with two actors each. Your best guess is that you can film everything in one day.

Start off with a spreadsheet outlining the line item, the cost, and how many you'll need. If you were shooting for more than 1 day, I would recommend adding an extra column in for days. But your spreadsheet should look something like this:

LINE ITEM	COST PER ITEM	# OF ITEMS	TOTAL COST

If you're an Excel or OpenOffice master (or simply a math wizard), you can probably figure out where this is going. We're going to make a spreadsheet that will tell us the total cost of everything, as well as the cost of each individual item.

Now we'll put a few basic formulas in so that when you type in a number, it *automagically* computes all of the mathematics for you! Below I've added fake cell numbers and letters so you'll easily be able to understand the formulas. Don't forget that every formula must start with the = sign.

	A	B	C	D
	LINE ITEM	COST PER ITEM	# OF ITEMS	TOTAL COST
1				
2	(item #1)	(enter individual item cost)	(enter # of items)	=2B*2C
3	(item #2)	(enter individual item cost)	(enter # of items)	=3B*3C
4	(*example*) Lights	$100	3	$300 (or =4B*4C)
5	(*example*) Microphone	$50	1	$50 (or =5B*5C)
6				
7	TOTALS	=SUM(2B:5B)	=SUM(2C:5C)	=SUM(2D:5D)

So, in this example, your totals should read:

7	TOTALS	$150	4	$350

That's it! Pretty simple, right? But depending on how many variables and options you're looking at, your budget can get pretty complicated pretty quickly. That's okay so long as you remember why you're budgeting: you need to add up how much everything is going to cost. If you have a better formula or a better way to do it, I encourage you to try that. This is all about making sure you have a good handle on what you have and what you need, so if something vastly simpler or incomprehensibly more complex is going to provide you the information you need, go for it.

For those of us who don't moonlight as production accountants, keep it simple. Just list everything you'll need and assign a price to it. It's really as simple as that. The only question now is, what do you need?

Sometimes you may be able to get away with just you and a camera and a chair. In that case I'd still recommend creating a budget, because little costs like office supplies, clothespins (called C-47's in the film world), and food will sneak up on you. If you don't have those listed out, you may run into trouble. I've been burned on food costs before, and believe me: pizza for the crew can add up quickly.

In other cases you may need to budget for an entire production crew, actors, equipment rentals, catering, even pets. Although I imagine you won't need to hire any jet pilots for your book trailer, maybe you will, and you should definitely account for those. You may need to pay an assistant director, or a camera operator, or an actress. You may need to budget for an editor or a graphic artist, or a sound technician. There are hundreds of different jobs and items that you need to consider accounting for when building a budget.

I must reiterate, however, that most likely *you will not need most of these line items.* The majority of book videos can be shot for free with you, a camera, and a couple of friends. If you do get more complicated, though, hopefully this list will help you.

That's great, you say, *but how will I know how much each thing costs?* Because that's what you really want to know: how much cashola must you dole out. The short answer is, simply, only as much as you want.

It is possible to find every resource you need for free, but in every market there is a standard price. For instance, for a professional-level production assistant in the film industry on the East coast in 2020, the average pay rate is $200-$300 per day for a 12-15 hour day. It may be more or less where you're from, and remember, that's for *professionals* working on *movies.* Prices are so often negotiable, it's impossible to tell you without knowing your situation.

Since I'm at severe risk of evading the question, I recommend you plan to spend around $500 in total, double that in a larger city. Yes, I know to most of you that sounds like a lot. Yes, you can do it for much cheaper. Yes, you can spend much, much more. Yes, you get what you pay for. And, yes, cash payment isn't always the best currency with people. Maybe you don't have to pay someone for the day, but you have to provide the finished product to them for their demo reel. Maybe they just want a signed copy of the book when it's published. Maybe they just think you're lovely and want to spend the day with you. There are all kinds of ways to beg, borrow and steal people and resources.

It's not like you're going to write a check for $500 and be done with it, either (well, not unless you hire a producer, which I will discuss later). Normally, it's not one lump sum. More than likely, you'll end up chipping away at expenses as you go, spending $5 here and $20 there over the course of a month or two. It doesn't feel like you're paying $500, but after a while, all of those little elements add up.

Now we come full circle, because you can see why it's important to have a budget! To keep from spending too much money on little things you didn't think about, be sure to think about them.

How to Make a Book Video for No Budget

So, as promised, let's see how you can make a book trailer for a $0 budget. I'm going to make a few assumptions in order to keep the price at $0, but will try to remain faithful to all non-film-professionals and what they may have available to them.

The first assumption is that you have, or have access to, the internet. In America today, internet access is so common I think it's a safe assumption that you have some sort of connection.

You'll also need access to some type of editing program, as well. The three most common professional editing programs are Adobe Premiere, Final Cut Pro (Mac only), and Avid. But they're not free, so for our $0 budget, let's assume you don't already have a program. No problem.

If you're a Mac person, iMovie comes standard on every Mac. For PC, I think there's some type of MovieMaker application, and you can always try to download something free online. You can also try a free version of DaVinci Resolve (Mac or PC), which has editing capabilities. There's a bit of a learning curve, though. There may even be a simple video editor in your app store, or even an online video editing program that you can use through your web browser. At the very least, I will have faith that you are a resourceful enough person to make friends with someone who has access to an editing program. The almighty Friend & Family Network is important here.

I'm also not going to include a meal in this estimate. If you're really stingy, grab something at Costco that's huge so you can feed everyone lunch for the price of just one. You could also try to get a local business to donate some food for your production, but it does involve a little bit of salesmanship. I've worked on projects fully catered by local restaurants in exchange for their name in the credits or a "special thanks" or similar co-marketing plan.

Another assumption is that you have friends or family.

Finally, I'll assume you're not going to be your worst enemy, and you will actually go out and try these things. I'm petty shy myself, so I understand the reservations and fears associated with doing something you're not familiar with, or worse, asking others to help you! But if you've already made the plan, it's surprisingly easy to get people to follow your lead. So the final assumption is that you're willing to lead.

To make our video for no cost, imagine you're planning on a script you've written with a narrator, two actors, some graphic text, two scenes or locations, and one day of filming.

The first thing to consider is your narrator. Let's go out on a limb and assume either you can narrate it yourself, or you can use the voice of one of your actors. You may also be able to find someone online via Voice123.com, Voices.com, Craigslist, or through any Google search for voice actors and databases. Be clear and honest about not being able to provide any money. You won't get a lot of hits, but you may be able to find a few voice actors hoping to beef up their voice demo reel who would be willing to give you a hand. Local voice actors often work on projects like this in exchange for demo reel material or a kind review on their website.

While we're on the subject of actors, let's find two on-screen actors for free. Begin with your network. For the sake of this example, we'll suppose you were able to find one ready and willing friend among your peers. For your second actor, you had to turn to your local film office, who hooked you up with a young actor who is just out of school and looking for some work to put on his/her demo reel. Perfect. You've just scored two $0 actors.

Now you've got to get the camera crew and equipment itself. To keep costs down, you will be the director, and maybe even the camera operator. I suggest that you find two people—a videographer with his/her own equipment and an audio tech with his/her own microphones—however you can find them. Later you'll see some tips and tricks for finding film pros, but for now just have the confidence that you can find two people. Even if you can't find the audio tech, that's okay, as most cameras have onboard microphones. It's not ideal, but it'll do. Either that, or don't have your actors speak.

So what will you do for lights and other production equipment? In the traditional film world the cameras were not very sensitive to light, and you needed large, expensive lights to make everything look right. Hollywood still uses hundreds of lights in any given movie, some so large they mimic the sun. But camera equipment has come a long way, and these days most consumer cameras produce excellent images with very little light. This means you can use *practical* lights, such as lamps, flood lights, and even light coming through windows to make your video look really good without needing to rent a truck full of thousands of dollars worth of lights. You'll have to get creative with the use of lights to make everything look they way you like (on low-budget projects we sometimes call this *"stylistic lighting"* as a joke), but you can create some incredible looks with just a window and a lamp.

The same goes for any camera equipment you may need. For instance, an old wheelchair works wonderfully as a dolly, you can place the camera on a towel on top of a desk to create another type of dolly, and you can generally McGyver just about anything you have lying around.

Now we'll need to find our shoot locations. In our case, you're looking for two separate places. Let's say one is outside and one is inside.

For your exterior (outside) set, we're going to assume you don't need to build anything like a huge castle or space ship, considering you followed my good advice and wrote a script that was feasible. First, of course, try your own property and any family and friends who might own what you're looking for. If you need something kind of scenic, try state parks. As long as you're not obstructing traffic or damaging the land, I've been assured by police officers and other officials that because it's public land, you're allowed to film there (within certain limits). You may be able to call in to the local police or ranger station and ask them what you can and can't do. In most states they're pretty friendly. You can also look for anywhere in the woods, fields, or pretty much anywhere that isn't private property. If you do need private property such as, say, a cornfield, and you don't have a friend who owns one, you may be able to simply knock on someone's door and ask permission. Most people are friendly and will even get excited about the project if you're nice to them. Remember that most people don't get to see a movie being made every day, so they may give you permission just so they can have bragging rights.

Once again, this depends on how well you treat others, and a little bit on where you live. California and NYC residents may meet more resistance because so many films and TV shows are shot in the area. Those big-budget projects usually pay for the use of a location.

If you need something in the city, that may actually be easier. Check with your local film office, but most of the time you don't need a permit or anything to film within the city so long as you're not on private property or impeding the flow of traffic. Some states have rules against light stands and things like that, but since you're traveling lean and mean, that probably won't be an issue. Just be sure to check, because some areas are very strict (Washington, DC is an example).

Once you find your city spot, I recommend talking to any businesses that may be nearby, or businesses that may end up in the shot, and let them know what's going on. It's courteous, it may mean less interruption during the shoot, and if you're really good you might even be able to convince one of the businesses that having their store in your book video is worth something to them. Who knows, maybe they'll offer to cater lunch in exchange for exposure in your trailer?

Finally, to avoid any headache, stay away from malls with major stores. Large, national stores tend to have much more stringent rules regarding where their store signs end up in videos, and even if you're on a public sidewalk they may come after you if you snag a large retail chain's logo in the shot. I've had this happen once or twice, even when we had permission from the city and the tourism council to be there—we even had a city representative with us—and we were promoting the mall, trying to pull in new visitors to the city. It didn't matter. They made us delete the footage. Stay away from malls.

If you absolutely have to, you can go "guerilla style." This means show up and hope for the best. I don't advocate this option because I think you should keep everything above board, and it's very embarrassing if you get shut down for disobeying some type of rule. But sometimes stealing the shot is the only way to get it. If you are going to go somewhere without permission, please be respectful of the property and please, please, be sure you and your crew are safe.

To find an interior shot, it's really the same bag of tricks. Start with your personal network and work your way out. The film office, once again, may be a wonderful resource for finding any type of location.

You need some graphic text next. Most video editing programs have the ability to create text. And since we've already assumed you can get your hands on an editing program, that may be it. If you need something a little fancier, you can download free Photoshop-like programs where you can create text in any kind of font, shape, size, etc. that you need. These programs are often "open source" or "freeware", and they're constantly updated or swapped out. By the time you read this, there may be new programs that haven't yet been invented, so keep an eye out for what the internet has created.

Another way to get what you need for free is, of course, by trying the same thing you tried to find video professionals. Editors and graphic artists and After Effects wizards are out there. Check with your friends, then your community, your film office, local schools, or online. You may be able to find some 3D animator and After Effects guru who is just dying to make some killer book video titles.

Now, all of this seems like it may take an awful lot of time, and it probably seems unrealistic to make this many connections just for a silly book video! But before you have a stroke, consider that you most likely will be able to get everything in a one-stop-shop. You might already have or know everyone you'll need. You might be able to tell someone at the film office what you're doing, and they find everything for you. You might happen to know a one-man-band who does it all. You might find that this was a whole lot simpler than what I've mentioned. This is just a list of ideas to get you started thinking. It is possible.

Whether or not you're spending pocket change or Scrooge McDuck bank vaults full of money, the point is to keep track of what you'll need and plan ahead. Budgeting is an important step in the creative preproduction process, and without it you may end up spending more money than you ever imagined. Or worse, you may end up with a book video that you don't like, because you weren't prepared.

Scheduling

Another important aspect of preproduction is the scheduling. For large productions such as movies and television shows, scheduling can get pretty complicated because of how many people and objects need coordinating. If you've got a room with 1,000 extras, Brad Pitt, a computer-generated monster attack, explosions, and jets that need to fly by all at the same time, you can see why scheduling is important.

For our purposes, however, you'll only need to get as detailed as you want with the schedule. The most basic schedule is simply stating which day you will film the video, what time you will start, what time you plan to end, and which day you plan to post the finished piece. Maybe that's all you need.

If you want to get a little bit more complex, which I always do, I suggest you focus on a **production schedule** and a **postproduction schedule**.

The production schedule maps out, in detail, your production day(s). If we use our two-scene example from before, this should include a shoot date, a call time (when your crew should arrive), a little bit of time for the camera crew to unload any gear and get set up, time for the actors to get into their costumes and do their makeup and hair, and a time you plan to start shooting. You should also probably have time scheduled for moving from one location to another, and setting up at the new location. Some schedules may even plan out each separate shot with an educated guess for how long each shot will take to get, down to the minute. That might be overkill for your purposes, however.

You can be as stringent or as loose with your schedule as you'd like, though I do recommend at the very least having a realistic plan for what time you'll start, what time you'll get lunch, and about what time you'll finish.

When creating a schedule, be realistic about how much time each part will take. If your actor has to put on a huge, complex costume, it doesn't do you any good to be overly optimistic about how long it will take them to get ready. You're not reporting your schedule to the union, so you might as well strive to make it accurate and plan plenty of time for each part of the day.

Much of this schedule can be reported on a **call sheet**. For professional productions, a call sheet is the main source of information for the day, including who is on the crew, contact information, set address, parking information, hospital locations, weather, and of course call times. If you're really into organizing like I am, it may be a fun exercise to make a professional call sheet. It also lends your shoot a touch of professionalism and makes you look really official if you do it right. Most likely, however, you don't need to send a call sheet for a book trailer. An email confirming the time and address where everyone should show up, along with your contact information if someone gets lost, will do just fine.

> **PRO-TIP**: *In that email, make sure everyone knows to **respond** to the email by highlighting, emboldening, italicizing, and increasing the font size of the word "respond."*

A ***post-production schedule*** is a schedule laid out in days or weeks that gives you an idea of how long it will take to edit and finish the video. If you know you're releasing your book on a certain date, and you plan to release the video on the same date, then you should probably make a note about it. The post-production schedule can also help you keep your ducks in a row if you have graphics, editing, text, music, and sound effects all happening at different times.

And this schedule doesn't have to be official or complex, either. Something as simple as noting that you expect to take 2 weeks to edit, 1 week to create the graphics, 1 day to find the perfect music, and 1 day to make any finishing touches before you release the video is probably all you'll need. If you're doing something more complicated and need to coordinate with people—say you have an animator creating a computer-generated monster—then having a realistic schedule for that person is going to be vital to smooth communication and making sure everything is finished on time.

Having a post-production schedule also keeps you from putting it off for months and months because there's no deadline. Give yourself and your team (if you have one) a clear end date to aim for. This will also reduce your stress and eliminate the feeling of having "that darn book trailer" hanging over your head for months because it just never seems to come to an end.

Location Scouting

It's kind of vital to the success of your video that you find out where exactly you're going to be filming the thing. Location and setting are extremely important for any type of video, especially if you're trying to create a certain mood. If your book video takes place in a bar, for instance, it behooves you to try to find a physical location that is the closest rendition of the bar you see in your head. This may require a little bit of effort on your part, as you're unlikely to own every location you'd want to use. You can start with your network of friends and family to see who owns or has access to a particular location you might want to shoot—maybe your buddy works at the perfect bar.

If you don't know or don't have access to the location you're looking for, a great place to start is your local film office. They often know plenty of local businesses that may be open to filming, and they may show you options you haven't before considered. A film office may also have access to an online community or email listserve where you can ask the entire film community if they have any resources.

If the film office seems to be a bigger bite than you're wanting to chew, the best and most direct way to secure a location is to ask the owner. Often times people who own or run businesses—especially bars, restaurants, shops, and other commercial locations—are open to allowing a film crew on their premises. They may have required hours, or request that you tweet about the location or include their logo in your video, or even require a 'location fee', but you'll never know until you ask. When approaching a business, keep in mind that the owner's primary goal is to make money. If you can find a way to convince them that you'll help them make more money, or at the very least won't cost them any, then you're on the right path.

Some locations may refuse to allow filming. If so, remain polite and accept that some areas are off limits. It's the nature of the beast. You may have to find another similar location, or build a set on your own. I've built spaceships in garages, created a gameshow on a theatre stage, turned a blank wall into a drug-dealer's office, and even filmed a muddy body burial in a suburban driveway. All this is to say, that when considering your location options, you should be creative and resourceful. Real locations may not suit your needs, and you may need to improvise to create your own.

> **PRO TIP**: *Remember that although you move and think in three dimensions, a video is flat. This means often you don't need an entire set, just one wall or maybe two. Remember that the only part of the set that needs to look authentic is what fits in the camera. No one will ever see what the lens isn't looking at.*

The process of searching for a shooting location and then viewing the available options is called **location scouting**. Gather information from your network and try to lock down a location to film that fits your vision for your video. This is another reason your schedule is so important, because if you need to rent a space, you'll want to make sure you know which day you'll be using it.

Once you've selected your favorite location(s), you should do a site survey or a **tech scout**, meaning you and anyone else who may need to see the space beforehand should visit the location to figure out a few things. Sometimes people refer to *this* as the location scout, but *potato/patato*. Typically you just want to see where there's available power or power outlets, lights, windows, doors, parking, whether there will be water, bathrooms, or a staging area to put gear that doesn't belong in the shot. You may want to keep it simple by assigning one person with a camera or camera phone to simply take and send pictures to anyone who needs to see the location beforehand.

Casting and Crewing: Finding Your Talent

Finding a cast and crew is essential to most live-action videos. It seems like a process best left to high-paid producers with nefarious connections throughout the surly depths of the film or criminal worlds, but even if you're no kingpin who can ensure somebody *never works in this town again*, you should be able to find the right people for your project.

As I've said so many times already, always begin with your network. Most likely you have a few friends who fit the roles nicely who were secretly thespians in high school. Try to get them to volunteer some time in exchange for, I don't know, walking their dog or something. You might even be able to lure people in simply by the chance to be in a book trailer. Often people find the prospect of appearing on screen exciting. My father got to be an extra in the background of a Hollywood movie 12 years ago, and he still talks about it today! Use the glamour to your advantage.

If you cannot find friends (or yourself!) to fit the roles, your next step would be to turn either to the community, your local film office, or the internet. Within the community, you're likely able to tap any kind of school resources, such as a local college with a film program or acting program. Ask the dean of that program for a few recommendations, or if she knows any students who may be interested. There may also be theatre coalitions in your town, or an improv acting troop. The thing about actors is that they tend to want opportunities to act, so you don't have to get a complex worrying about asking people to do something they'd rather not do. Just remember that, more often than not, you get what you pay for. It's unlikely you'll discover the next Oscar winner willing to work for free. But you never know.

Your next stop should be your local film office. Although they may or may not give you the time of day, if you're confident your book video—and your book—will be a success and you can sell them on the idea that their office or locale will gain valuable exposure, they may put you in touch with casting agents who know of actors hungry enough to work for free. One of the main functions of any film office is to ensure that video production happens within their jurisdiction, so they are usually willing to help anyone who approaches them with a legitimate project. You may also be able to approach casting agents or agencies directly and ask if they have anyone who might be interested in acting in a book video for copy/credit/reel. This is more likely to work in areas that are not already well known for filmmaking. In New York or Los Angeles you're unlikely to get a response from the film office or professional agencies. However, you'd be surprised at the responses you'll get from the internet.

To find your local film office or any film-related programs, a quick internet search should yield any results you're looking for. Not every town is going to have its own film office, but just about any state should. Even if they're tucked way back into the inner workings of the local government, there's more than likely someone who can answer your questions about filmmaking in your area.

If face-to-face networking isn't getting you anywhere, and your film office doesn't pan out, there are several online options you can try. First, make sure there is not already an existing online database for film production. For example, if you're around the Virginia/DC/Maryland area, the Mid-Atlantic Production Guide has just about every working professional listed. Another simple and straightforward way to find people (perhaps not yet established as professionals) is to post an "ad" to a site like Craigslist, Mandy.com, or other listservs. These are large databases and public forums where actors (and others) tend to look for posts about projects they could get involved in. Much like a community bulletin board, except accessible from anywhere.

When posting an ad, be sure to mention when the shoot is, what you're looking for, whether or not you're paying (if not, typically you'd write "copy, credit, and meals"), and how they can get in contact with you. You should also ask for a headshot, or even an audition if you think that's necessary. At the very least, a headshot and resume should come with any responses you get, so you know what the actor looks like.

Posting to online public forums is inherently fraught with danger and obstacles, and each response you get should come with an asteroid-sized grain of salt, but be not daunted. You can first try Facebook and look for any acting or filmmaking groups in your area. This is a great resource to find those who are just starting in the industry and looking for opportunities to show off their skills. Just be aware most likely the big-time pros don't use these resources because they already have a network of guy-who-knows-a-guy.

Check with acting or filmmaking meet-up groups on meetups.com, or even post on Craigslist.org. You might be able to host a Meetup for local filmmakers in your area and pitch them your idea. They might want to help you just for the experience! Your local film office may have a hotline or a message board where you can post acting opportunities, and there may be other filmmaking associations in your area that notify others of opportunities. Here in Virginia, we have the Virginia Production Alliance, Women in Film and Video, TIVA-DC, and the Virginia Film Office Hotline. Just to name a few. Your city or state probably has something similar.

Don't forget that narrators are actors, too. In addition to everything you'd try to find an actor, you can also find online databases of voice actors who may record and post an audition for your video. You can try sites like voice123.com or voices.com. There are many, many others to check out as well. It all starts with a quick search with your favorite internet browser.

Finally, if you have money and a few connections, or a very silver tongue, you can try local talent agencies or even casting directors. Depending on the size of your town and the resources it has, you may have a few talent agents who would be open to casting your project for you. Just be sure to be clear about any costs involved and what you are/are not allowed to do with the actors.

Casting and Crewing: Finding Your Crew

Equally important to finding actors is the camera crew and equipment. If you have your own camera, whether it's a video camera or a DSLR, then you're set unless you need more advanced equipment. Typically, you want to stay away from a camera that doesn't have a lens that you can detach, unless it's a specific type of video camera. The specific camera options are too numerable to list, and change constantly. For your purposes, if you don't own a DSLR and aren't interested in doing intense research about camera technology, you might want to consider finding someone who already knows their stuff.

If you don't have access to a camera, you should be on the lookout for a director of photography (also called DP, cinematographer, or videographer) who has their own equipment. Once again start with your network. Have a friend from college who used to always film the sorority recruitment video? Reach out to her and see if she's interested. Know someone who is a photographer and might be able to point you in the right direction, or may want to try his hand at video? Give him a call. Tell your friends what's going on and what you're looking for, and you're likely to find someone who knows someone.

From there, work your way towards many of the same resources you'd check for actors. This includes the film office, Facebook, Mandy.com, Meetups, etc. Once you've found your crew, it's important to be respectful of people's time and personalities, especially since you're most likely asking them to work for you for free. If you need a crew, always remember that these are professionals (or future professionals) who typically make their living by doing this. If they're willing to help you for free, that is a huge favor, and they deserve your respect. You wouldn't do your day job for free, would you?

Keep in mind, also, that since you're going for a full day of production, you will have to feed everyone. For this reason, I recommend trying to keep your crew as small as possible without sacrificing quality—it may even just be you.

Suiting up for Production

Once you've completed all of these steps you should have a really good idea of what your book video will look like once it's done. That's why the saying "the movie is made in preproduction" is so accurate. If you've done your homework and your preproduction is solid, you should feel confident going into production with a clear idea of what you want and the skills to pull it off.

> **PRO TIP**: *Organize everything in one of those plastic accordion binders. It's incredibly helpful to have one place with all of your plans and paperwork.*

For many people, however, all the planning in the world won't get rid of the nerves associated with undertaking a book video or leading a team. That's okay—it's even natural. Have faith in yourself and your abilities, and do your best to stick to the plans you've developed in the preproduction stage.

Now that you've gotten everything planned, scheduled, lined up and ready to go, the actual production—the film shoot—should be easy. It's basically paint-by-the-numbers. Right?

Right?

Production: Where Everyone Thinks the Magic Happens

Well, not exactly. No matter how much planning you've done, things always, always, *always* change once you begin filming. The most important thing about filming is to be flexible, and roll with the punches. Finding that fine line between simply going with the flow and becoming an uncompromising, over-managing, insufferable dictatorial diva is what production is all about. That's how you capture the magic.

In this chapter I'm going to explain how to actually shoot your book trailer in a way that maximizes that magic. I'm also going to mention some tips and tricks that will improve your video's quality tenfold, although remember this isn't a filmmaking manual. I'd rather focus on what you'll need to make a halfway decent video to advertise your *book*. You can find the filmmaking basics by searching Youtube, Yahoo, Vimeo, Bing, Google or even (gasp) the library. I wouldn't be able to explain those concepts better than those who've already done it.

I can, however, provide an introduction and a guideline for those of you who aren't interested in pursuing a career as the next great American film director. If you're here to make your book video knock some serious socks off of your contemporaries, this chapter is going to help you. This is where the rubber meets the road; the piano meets the sidewalk; the match meets the fuse. This is also the part of the process everyone associates with "making a movie". Let's dive in, what do you say?

Prepping and Rehearsal

Once you've gotten everyone in place, the actors are getting ready, and the crew is standing around wondering what to do, it's time you let everyone else in on exactly how this scene will come together. Go through the scene, or the shot, one more time with everyone who needs to know. Show them exactly where to stand, what to do, and explain briefly what you're going for. Then rehearse it.

Rehearsals help everyone, because it lets the actors and the crew know where everything is going to be, how it is spaced out, and what resources they may use. If you're rigging lights or trying to pull off a camera move, the rehearsal will help the crew coordinate this move, or at least see where they can put the lights.

The rehearsal also allows your actors to learn where they should stand, how they should walk, and ask any questions they may have, such as what to do with their hands. Your job is to patiently guide them through that, so when the camera is running, everything else is clockwork.

Even if your book video is just you and a friend, it will help to at least "go over the plan" one more time before turning the camera on. You'll find that the filming goes quickly and is much more fun once you've seen a rehearsal.

How to Shoot (a Camera)

This is where I'm going to get into a few specifics for you. You see, most people can figure out how to hold a camera, turn it on, and point it at something. But that's simply not enough, and there's a reason photography and filmmaking are considered arts—it requires a delicate combination of skill, knowledge, and plain old-fashioned magic.

If you want your book trailer to look and feel better than the abysmal average, you should aim for excellence when shooting it. The camera work is where you can really make your video shine, and sadly it's where most people go horribly, terribly, and sometimes hilariously wrong.

Why is it so important? Camera work is an instant indicator of quality. It's usually subtle and for some may even be subliminal, but the composition of your shots creates a bias within the viewer's mind. That bias encompasses how they perceive the story, the quality of the product as a whole, and even the skill of the writer. A person may not even know why, but if they watch a book trailer with bad cinematography, they may feel the book is poorly written. The image is vital.

So allow me to offer you a few tips and tricks that will improve your composition, camera moves, and may even impact the quality of any picture you take for the rest of your life. Think of all the wonderful home videos you can make!

Composition

Most people think movies are made with someone simply picking up a camera and pointing it at the action. But if that were true, we'd all get bored or motion sick after five minutes, and movies would be an oddity, not the cultural nuclear bombs that they are. So *where* and *how* you point that camera are incredibly important. This is known as the **composition** of the shot.

If you've taken a 'Basics of Photography' class in high school or college, or even watched a few videos online, much of this may sound pretty familiar to you, but humor me. The composition of each shot—or each "cut", or each "clip"—is important and deserves more thought than just point-and-shoot logic.

A **shot**, as I'm defining it here, is one instance of time in your film where the camera is in a certain place and records a certain action. Several shots make up a larger action, such as a conversation or walking from the door to the refrigerator and back. This larger action, or several actions, makes up a scene. A **scene**, visually, is where something happens in a certain location, usually from beginning to end, though not always.

To illustrate this, let's imagine a full scene, and break it down into its components. Here's your script:

INT. SALLY'S KITCHEN – NIGHT
SALLY stands in fear at the edge of the counter. JOE is stepping towards the refrigerator.

                                SALLY:

> Don't open it, whatever you do.
> **JOE**:
> Well, how dangerous could it be? It's just a fridge.
>
> *Joe turns away from her, crosses the kitchen, and opens the fridge. He sees nothing inside. He turns back to face Sally.*
> **JEO**:
> See? Nothing's th—
>
> *A moldy ARM reaches from the refrigerator and grabs Joe's shoulder.*
> **CUT TO BLACK.**

That's a scene because it takes place in the same location, it has a start and an end, and is composed of one or more actions. In this case, the actions include the initial conversation, crossing the room, opening and looking into the fridge, and finally the hand grabbing Joe.

To accomplish each of these actions, you may need several shots. For instance you'll probably want a wide shot—called the **establishing shot**—to show where each character is standing, the kitchen, and to give the audience an idea of the space. For the conversation, you'll then most likely want a shot of Sally's face when she's talking, and a shot of Joe's face when he's talking. In the edit you can line these shots up back-to-back to create a sequence that looks like it's all happening chronologically. This is called **continuity editing**, and I'll touch on that a little later in post-production.

For a book trailer, you may not need an entire scene. You might just need one or two shots of something, just enough to communicate that there are exciting plot points in your book. Either way, the composition of each shot is still going to be important.

There are books and articles and blogs and vlogs and rhyming mnemonic devices galore that go into the finer details and philosophy of shot composition, but for the average person, I'll try to simplify.

Firstly, there is a bit of terminology to use. You're probably familiar with it already, but just in case, the three most basic shots are called the **wide shot**, **medium shot**, and **close shot** (or close-up). And they're exactly like they sound. A wide shot typically shows a person head-to-toe, or a broad view of a location, landscape, or scene. Almost every establishing shot is a wide shot, because it *establishes* the setting. A medium shot is a little trickier to nail down, but it's basically a shot that is framed so that a person's lower half isn't visible. This may mean from the thigh to the head, or belly to head, or simply the middle ground between what you think is a wide shot of an object and what you think would be considered a close shot.

> **PRO TIP**: *Notice how I didn't say to frame them from the knees up or the waist up? That's because you want to try to avoid framing people by cutting them off at natural joints. Subconsciously the viewer sees that as strange.*

If you're filming people, a close shot is typically the head and shoulders, much like a studio portrait. If you're getting even closer, say really close to the person's eye, this is called an **extreme close up**. There is much more to it, but these are the basics, and will help you communicate your vision. It's also important to remember when filming a book video that *not every shot has to be a medium*.

The Rule of Thirds

The next most important part about framing a shot correctly is to follow what is known as the ***Rule of Thirds***. This is the almighty principle that guides almost every photograph or moving image you'll see—except the rare instances when the shot needs to be symmetrical for dramatic purposes. I would say 98% of every single movie, trailer, photograph, graphic, or other professional image you're likely to see adheres to the Rule of Thirds. If you're a mathematician or get really jazzed about the Fibonacci Sequence, the Rule of Thirds is closely related to the golden ratio. We're talking blood relatives, probably twins.

But for those not inclined towards the mathematics, have no fear, it's really easy. Image your TV screen. It's a horizontal rectangle, right? Imagine it were divided into three equal parts horizontally, and vertically. Your screen would look something like this:

When you compose a shot, or "frame it up", whatever is the most important part of that shot, the part you want your audience to see, should fall upon one of those intersections. If filming a person, for instance, their eyes are the most important part and thus almost always fall on an intersection of two lines. If you're filming a wide shot of a ship, you'll notice that the deck is lined up with one of the horizontal lines. If you're filming just about anything, your shot will always look just a little more professional if it's framed up according to the Rule of Thirds. But don't take my word for it. Put tape over your TV and go watch your favorite movie. I guarantee a majority of the shots will have the subject lined up along one of the lines of thirds.

But there are so many great shots where the subject is in the center! you proclaim. And this is true. However, that is almost always for dramatic purposes and is more of a Level 2 lesson. If you see a shot that simply blows you away by centering the subject, go for it! But when in doubt, follow the Rule of Thirds. Also, keep an eye on *all* of the 1/3 lines. Notice anything? Yes, even that famous shot of the villain sitting atop the throne that is centered in the middle of the castle follows the Rule of Thirds if you look closely. Where are the villain's eyes? You guessed it. I'd bet you dollars to donuts his eyes fall along that upper horizontal line. I bet there are even pillars of stone on either side of the throne that line up perfectly with the vertical lines. See what I mean? The Rule of Thirds, that sneaky golden ratio, is just about everywhere.

But it's not the only thing to consider when framing a shot. You'll also want to look at your **headroom** and your **lead room**.

Headroom and Lead Room

Headroom doesn't exactly have a hidden meaning. It is the distance between the top edge of the frame and your subject's top surface. With people, this means the top of their head. If there is too much headroom—which is a common mistake—it will look like the person is unusually short, and the shot will look unbalanced and strange, like there's too much dead space. That's because, well, there *is* too much dead space. Most likely if you have too much head room, that means the person's eyes aren't on the upper 1/3rd line, but rather more towards the middle. Tilt the camera down until there's only a little bit of headroom and the eyes fall right within the Rule of Thirds guidelines.

Sometimes the shot may be so close or at such an angle that if you were to allow for headroom, the bottom of the face would be cut off. In this case, rely on your rule of thirds, and keep the eyes on that top line.

Headroom works in the opposite way as well—you don't want too little headroom, because then it looks like the top of the person's head is stuck to the edge of the frame and they're just hanging in space. Make sure you leave a little bit of breathing room between the top of the frame and the top of your subject's head.

Lead room is a directional cue, and helps you decide on which side of the screen to place your subject. Think of it like this; if a bicycle is riding across the screen from left to right, you should have more space in front of the bicycle than behind it. Essentially, you're leading the bicycle and allowing your viewer's eyes room to keep up with the motion. If you're moving the camera, the same idea applies. Move the camera so that there is always room in front of your subject, whether it is moving or static. So if you're trying to keep that bicycle in frame by following it, make sure it stays on the left side of the screen.

Lead room also applies to people in conversation. In most cases, a person on screen is rarely staring straight at the camera. Rather, she is looking off to one side. When you frame your shot, try to leave plenty of room in front of her, so she's looking into the negative space, rather than looking at the edge of the frame. This helps keep the frame from appearing cluttered or uncomfortable.

Depth of Field

Another major consideration when composing a shot is the **depth of field**. This is a fairly technical and complicated concept if you want to get into the nitty-gritty of it (there's math involved—*eck!*), but basically think of it in terms of how blurry your background is. Most people associate movies with shots of beautiful people talking while the background is mostly out of focus. This is called **shallow** *depth of field,* because only the subject is in focus and there doesn't appear to be any depth to the frame. This is typically used for close ups of people or objects.

Sometimes you may want a wide shot of the landscape or cityscape, something that you believe the viewer's eye should wander through to pick up all of the details in the middle ground and background. For this you'll want a **deep** *depth of field.* The name comes from the idea that you can look into the frame and see clearly deep into the distance.

You may want to adjust your depth of field to achieve a certain look, thus making your images more "cinematic". There are some simple tricks (and some not-so-simple) to adjusting depth of field. Depth of field comes from a relationship between the iris, the shutter speed, the focal length, and the distance between subject and background.

Typically a wide open iris and more than ten feet between subject and background will create that shallow depth of field that so many people associate with a cinematic image. To adjust the depth of field, play around with your iris (this is the f-stop value, the aperture, or that funny decimal written on your lens, like 2.8). Typically, the lower that number, the shallower your depth of field is. Be aware that the lower that number, the more light the lens lets in (brighter image).

Another simple tactic to create a shallow depth of field is to back up and zoom in. That's right, it's usually that simple for most cameras and zoom lenses. If you have a prime lens (it doesn't zoom), this won't help much, though. Zooming in increases your focal length and typically shrinks your depth of field, emphasizing the distance between subject and background. If all of that sounds like nerd-speak, don't worry. Just try it out and you'll see what I mean. You don't need to know the terminology to frame a shot that you like.

If you have several different lenses, then the longer the lens (focal length), the more likely you will be able to achieve a shallow depth of field. You can check the length of your lens by looking for the number in millimeters. Typically lenses that are good for close ups are 50mm, 75mm, 85mm, and higher. If you're looking for a wide shot, you want a lens below 50mm. If you have a zoom lens, typically it will say on the lens which focal lengths you can zoom to. For instance, you may have a 40-135mm zoom lens, meaning you can zoom in and out to create a focal length anywhere between 40mm and 135mm.

There is another reason you may want a shallow depth of field. You know those cool shots in the movies where the focus goes from one person in the foreground and then moves to a person in the background? Like if you have a monster blurry in the background behind your actor, you can shift the focus from the actor to the monster, creating a scare. This is called a **rack** *focus*. You achieve this by simply spinning the focus wheel from one subject to the next. It creates a really engaging effect, and it's fun to do!

Basic Shooting Tips

Finally, when it comes to composing the shot, I want to share some quick advice if you're a newcomer to using a camera. These are guidelines and can be broken once you know what you're doing, but following these basic rules helps you avoid embarrassing mistakes and capture useful, watchable images.

First, use a tripod. The difference between films with steady shots and films with handheld shots is dramatic, because camera shake is annoying. Yes, shaky camera is used all the time in films for dramatic effect, but it is used carefully. When less experienced shooters don't have their camera on a tripod, the result quickly makes the viewer queasy. Think of all those terrible vacation videos your parents shot and you refuse to watch because you can't follow the action. Yeah. Don't do that.

Keep your hand off of the zoom. This is my personal pet peeve, and today zooming is regarded almost entirely as unacceptable in a movie. Amateur filmmakers, vacationers, and idiots tend to think zooming in and out over and over is a good idea, and it is not! Not ever! Not slowly, not quickly, not for dramatic effect, not for anything. Keep your hand off the damn zoom while you're recording. It's as simple as that, and I can't stress it enough. Zooming, if done well, is cheesy and lazy at best. Most of the time it is simply disastrous. Do. Not. Zoom.

You'll also want to keep direct sunlight out of your lens. Sometimes you may want an artsy lens flare or sunset shot, yes, but in general having sun in your shot is going to make everything too bright and can give your images a milky look or annoying flares that shouldn't be there. Shading your lens can make a dramatic difference when it comes to handling sunlight and getting the shot you want.

Some of you may be filming things on your phone. This is nothing to be embarrassed about, and today's phone cameras can capture some excellent, crisp images. Keep in mind, however, that you should always film horizontally (long-ways). This way you won't have black bars on either side of your video when you go to edit it together. If you hold your phone vertically (like you probably do normally when taking a picture), when the film goes up on Youtube or Vimeo or wherever, it is going to look unprofessional and most likely won't be very popular. Turn your phone sideways and you'll have achieved the right aspect ratio.

You may have the option to shoot in different frame rates (fps), such as 23.98, 24, 29.97, 30, 59.97, 60, or higher. Typically, movies are shot in 23.97 or 24 frames per second. This has to do with how many photos are taken per second and how much motion blur is created. Physical, old school film has a certain look to it, and 24 frames per second creates that same "film" look. There are reasons for choosing different frame rates, but there's no need to go into them. Whichever frame rate you choose, you'll want to shoot in the same frame rate for each shot, i.e. don't have some shots in 24fps and some in 30fps. If you don't, you may face problems when you edit the footage. If your camera doesn't have any frame rate options, it's not the end of the world. Most cameras nowadays are such high quality that it won't matter.

Finally, be careful with slow motion. Unless you understand frame rates and the process behind over-cranking and how to make everything appear slow in the edit, you may want to reconsider slow motion. In particular, you don't want to slow down footage too much in the edit unless it was shot specifically for slow motion.

> **PRO TIP**: *If the numbers and frame rates and aspect ratios and formatting options are confusing, here's the most common way to set up your camera. Select a frame rate of 23.98fps or 24fps, and a file size of 1920x1080 High Definition. This will produce the most common professional image out there without necessitating too much camera operation knowledge.*

How to Move the Camera

One of the things that sets apart professional video from amateur video is camera movement. Those sweeping cinematic shots, those dramatic dolly shots, those car chase scenes, and yes, even those shaky fight scenes all help to increase the power of your images.

But it's *how* you move the camera that makes everything look so cinematic. As previously mentioned, rule numero uno is, *keep your hands off of the zoom*. This bears repeating, so I'll repeat it: *don't use the zoom*. Part of the reason I'm such a stickler about this is because zooming shots look amateur. And you want to look professional. You've spent your hard-earned time and money and most of your sanity taking your writing career into the professional sphere. Don't slack when it comes to advertising for your book. Don't let it look cheap.

To wit: try to get a few camera moves in there. It doesn't have to cost anything, there don't have to be many, and they don't have to be major technical achievements. In fact, many of your shots are going to be beautiful *because* they're steady and don't move.

For those that need a little extra drama or action, try it. Simple things like panning with the action or *smoothly* following a character's head from one side of the screen to the other can really make an astounding difference.

If you want to get even more dramatic, be not deterred! There are many ways to make interesting, dynamic shots that move. For smooth dolly shots you can use a wheelchair, or a skateboard, or an office chair, or someone filming out of the open door of a minivan. I've even seen a moving shot made from placing the camera on a newspaper and sliding that newspaper (carefully) across a table.

You can get creative with crane shots by, you know, using a crane. Or you can try tying the camera to a rope and using a pulley (I recommend some trial and error before strapping your camera to a pulley, though...), or locking the camera to an improvised "selfie stick" to swing it around in a smooth arch of motion.

With today's constantly evolving drone technology, you can achieve some even more dynamic moves with remote-controlled drones. Not strictly aerials, either. You can capture some excellent crane shots and dolly shots with drones as well. Just be sure the FAA—or your insurance company—doesn't come knocking after you've flown your drone. I always recommend being current on the drone regulations, as they tend to change with the tides.

No matter what you imagine or how you execute it, remember that the goal is almost always smooth, fluid motion. These motions help create atmosphere, emphasis, and better communicate ideas. It is like making visual music. Move the camera and find something beautiful.

How to Light

Lighting really deserves its own chapter—heck, it deserves the hundreds of books already written about it—but for the sake of brevity I'll give you the quick-and-dirty rundown when it comes to lighting your videos.

The first rule is to *use lights*. Many cameras today are very good at capturing images in low lighting, but they're not *that* good. You can almost never have too many lights. That's because your goal isn't merely about seeing the images, it's about painting with the light to create a mood. Lighting matters to video as much as word choice matters to writing.

I don't mean to sound aristocratic or overly artsy when I say you should be painting with light. Rather, consider that each shot you capture is essentially a picture, and you should get the most out of that picture you can. Different color lights create moods, can help with effects, and can even help take your shot from ho-hum to friggin' sweet simply by separating your characters from their background.

The basics of lighting are centered around the idea of **three-point lighting**. This means—you guessed it—there are three lights. Namely, the **key light**, the **fill light**, and the **backlight**.

The **key light** is your main light. It illuminates the main characters in a desired way. Usually this is a large, soft light. In most cases you want to avoid harsh shadows. To make that key light have softer shadows, you can back it off, bounce it off of a white surface (like a wall or a ceiling), or put some type of non-flammable material in front of it. That's referred to as diffusing the light, and it takes your light source and gives it the appearance of a natural light, rather than a harsh spotlight. You typically place your key light slightly off to one side, and have it shining on the most important subjects.

Directly opposite the key light, behind your characters and shining on the backs of their heads, you will put your **backlight**. This is also referred to sometimes as a hair light or rim light, and it serves to create contrast between your subject and their background. It creates a separation that is typically pleasing to the eye, while the light itself is usually framed out of the shot. Backlights typically work best when they are above the subject, shining down on their hair. This is what makes everyone on TV looks like they have a little bit of a halo, and shiny, clean hair.

Finally, use a **fill light** to brighten up the shadows on the opposite side of the frame. In other words, if your key light is illuminating the right side of your character's face, there may be a harsh, dark shadow on the left side of their face. To counteract this, you use a fill light to fill in those shadows with a little more light. The fill light is usually softer and dimmer than the key light, and creates that third source of light in our three-point lighting scheme.

Lighting Interviews and Testimonials

Three-point lighting is also typically used for on-screen testimonials, so if you're shooting an interview or getting a sound bite from an expert, you're typically going to want a three-point lighting situation.

Another thing to consider is creating a *catch light*, also known as an eye light. By shining light into the character's eyes, it creates bright white dots in their pupils. This makes characters look intelligent, beautiful, and alive. You can usually adjust your key light until you see the reflection in your subject's eyes, and then you can tweak from there. Just be sure not to blind your actors.

You don't have to go out and spend thousands of dollars on expensive film lights unless you really, really want to. Household items, lamps, flood lights, fluorescent bulbs, even Christmas lights or paper lights all work really well as lighting fixtures. You can get creative with what you have, and remember that necessity is the mother of all invention—even when it comes to clever lighting.

Of course we could delve into more advanced lighting schemes like five-point lighting and overhead studio lighting and all kinds of things, but the truth is that every situation is different. Sometimes you may want an extra light in the background to illuminate an important object or cast a different color on the back wall. Sometimes you might want to fake the glow of a television screen or a fireplace. Sometimes you may want a practical light in the shot, such as a lamp. Maybe you even want only one overhead light for an intense police interrogation shot. Whatever the use, try to keep an eye on what is illuminated and what isn't. It will make a huge difference in the appearance of your footage.

Acting

If at all possible, make sure your actors are good. This may be a tall order, but nothing ruins a project faster than poor acting. Many times if the acting in a movie is bad enough it will show through even in the trailer, so be conscious of this. If you have really strong performances for the most part, but have a few lines that flop over dead, for Pete's sake use the good performances in your video, and cut the bad lines!

As the producer (and probably the director), the ultimate responsibility of the success of your video comes down to you. Actors often need direction, and that means they need you to tell them what you want to see. Be patient and help them. They *want* to do a good job, and that means they *want* to please the director. With that in mind, tell them how they can do that.

If there are no good performances, you may have a problem. However, you may not. You can—and should—make an awesome video even with poor performances. Maybe spice it up with some b-roll, or text, or slow motion? If the actors can't carry the weight of the video, you'll have to rely on everything else to do that. Sometimes it works, sometimes it doesn't. Err on the side of caution and find actors who are convincing.

Directing

Aside from the camera work, much of the quality of your final product depends on your direction. The crew, the actors, and eventually the audience are all looking to you for some direction. I'm not saying you have to be Spielberg or J. J. Abrams, but leading your crew and communicating with them is essential.

Directing is more than just calling "action" and "cut". You're the one with the vision, the man with the plan, the hostess with the mostest. If you're using actors, they're going to look to you when they don't know what to do. If you're interviewing experts, those experts are going to expect you to ask relevant questions and put them at ease so they look good. Being a director has a lot to do with gaining the trust of your crew, your actors, or your interview subjects. If they're convinced you're worth helping, they're going to open up and give you what you need. Sometimes all you need to do is ask.

You often hear horror stories about Hollywood directors yelling at people, throwing desks, and making actors cry. That may be acceptable on big budget movies (actually, it isn't anymore), but it certainly isn't going to get anything accomplished on a low/no budget video. Remember that directing like that is a lot like being a school bully. No one actually likes you, and they're only going to do the bare minimum until they can leave.

When working with everyone, be cordial, patient, and confident without being demeaning. Remember that the people you're working with may not see exactly what you do in your head, so your goal is to guide them into creating what you need. Respect will serve you much better than arrogance and tyranny.

Most likely you'll be using folks who aren't, strictly speaking, professional actors, so there are a few quick guidelines for them to follow. First, train them not to look at the camera! The camera lens tends to be a magnet for the uninitiated, so be sure to keep an eye on anyone's stray glances. You don't want to edit the video together and notice your background extra glaring right at the camera. It's unsettling.

Give the actors some motivation, or 'business'. In other words, something to do with their hands and their bodies other than just stand there. If you watch most TV shows or movies you'll notice there are rarely long conversations with two people standing in front of each other talking. Usually one person moves around, or fiddles with something, or is cooking or cleaning or whatever. This is as much for the benefit of the actors as it is for the story, because it gives them something to do that feels natural.

Give them some underlying tension if you're trying to get a little more out of their performance. There are several little scenarios you can run to create some underlying feeling to a scene. For instance, if you've got two people having a conversation, have them say their lines and move around as if they're flirting or trying to seduce one another. That little bit of cat-and-mouse can add to a scene. Or maybe have one of them keep trying to get close to the other, and the other keep backing away. You can have each of them trying to sneak an object off the desk while the other doesn't notice. Or tell them both to say each line as if they meant the opposite of what they're saying.

All of this may be a non-issue for you, however, since you're making a commercial and won't likely have full scenes. You may not have actors at all! Who knows what you'll need to show off your book? Just don't forget about communicating with the people who are helping you, whether it's a crew of two or two hundred.

Conducting Interviews

There's a strong likelihood you will need to conduct an on-camera interview of someone (or have someone interview you). The idea of this on-screen testimonial style is to give some sincerity and heart to your message. This is particularly helpful when trying to promote non-fiction, although there may be amazing ways to promote your fiction with this style as well, such as a fake documentary (think of "The Blair Witch Project" or "District 9" or even "Borat").

In the last ten years I've conducted thousands of on-camera interviews, and I've picked up on a few basics that I can share with you here. These aren't hard and fast rules, but when in doubt you can start here.

When framing an interview, most times you don't want your subject looking directly at the lens. Rather, have them look slightly off to one side of the lens. If you're asking the questions, have them look at you as if having a conversation. This serves a dual purpose; making the interview appear less direct and more heartfelt, as well as helping your subject feel less anxious about being on camera.

Most likely, you'll want a documentary-style interview where the final product will not include the questions or the person asking them. Rather, once edited together, the final video will appear as if the person on camera is spontaneously explaining things to the audience. You'll want to avoid a news-like interview—with one microphone going back and forth between interviewer and interviewee—as that can get rather boring visually. Let your interview subject know this up front, that you'll be taking bits and pieces from what they've said and stringing them together to form a complete thought.

The goal of a successful interview is to have a conversation, rather than a prepared statement. Thus, try your best not to let your subject think too much about the answers to the questions beforehand. Often people will try to rehearse a prepared speech and it comes off stilted and robotic and, worst of all, unconvincing and insincere. Rather, have them say spontaneous things, use slang, talk with their hands, show you their personality.

Prep your interview subject by asking them to answer your questions in complete sentences. For instance, if you ask their favorite color, they shouldn't just say, "blue", but rather, "my favorite color is blue."

Try to avoid asking yes or no questions. Rather, ask open-ended questions like "what are you most proud of?" or "what is the most interesting part about this subject?" That way their answers will be self-contained and able to stand on their own, rather than answers to a question viewers won't know you've asked.

Encourage your subject to try and avoid phrases like, "as I said before" or "as you were saying". This is because the final video may not be in chronological order, and, again, the audience won't see the questioner or hear the questions.

If you're asking the questions, keep your questions brief, and use silence to your advantage. The police often use this tactic when trying to milk a confession out of a subject. When your subject finishes talking, wait a few seconds. Most people tend to want to fill that silence with more information, and that's usually where the good stuff is. They'll follow up on what they've said or delve deeper into what they meant. Sometimes they'll even cry. That's when you know you've gotten some golden footage!

With regards to the way everything looks, there are a few steps you can take to put people at ease and make your interview stand out from the nightly news interviews. First, hide the microphones. This includes the lavaliere mics (the little clip-on ones). Hide them under a collar, beneath a shirt, even in your subject's hair. There's no excuse for showing off the microphone.

If you're a *really* considerate person, use bounce cards to bounce light onto your subject's face rather than shining lights in their faces. This may also help with any squinting issues. You can be even more considerate by bringing tissues or napkins to wipe sweat away from your subject, or even bring your own makeup. Ask permission before getting in someone's face, though.

Give your subjects some guidance regarding what to wear. In particular, tell them to avoid any brand names or shirts with large words (unless it's their company's logo or something). Typically pure white or pure black are problematic, and they should try to avoid whacky patterns or really small, close stripes.

Finally, when asking questions, remember that every story is about *people* and how they *feel*. Even the most boring, technical mumbo-jumbo can be enthralling if there are engaging personalities explaining it. To do this, frame your questions in a way that touches on how the person feels, what they're proud of, what they're scared of, challenges they face, challenges they've overcome, philosophies on life and love and anything that people hold dear to themselves.

On-Set Audio

Most likely, your trailer will feature some type of sounds or words captured during production. Whether these are lines from a scene, sound effects, or narration, you want to pay close attention to what you're hearing. Sound should be recorded and recorded well, because the importance of audio cannot be overstated.

In film school, they have us watch the same scene in two ways: once with just the visuals, once with just the audio and a blank screen. It's nearly impossible to watch a movie with only the visual part, but you can follow a scene almost entirely based on just the audio tracks. *That* is how important audio is.

And there aren't too many ways to fake good audio, either. So it behooves you to get it right.

Obviously, my first recommendation is to buy or rent good quality microphones, a professional audio technician, and have your performers perform on a sound stage so you have crisp, clear audio. That's most likely cost prohibitive, though, so here are some basic precautions you can take to ensure better audio.

"Quiet on set" is not just a cliché. It is important that your background crew, friends, workers, or even gawkers remain quiet the entire time the camera is rolling. The reasons for this go without saying. I only mention it because you'd be surprised how many people will *keep talking* if they don't think the camera is pointed at them.

On-camera microphones rarely produce acceptable audio, so do your best to get an external microphone. Keep that microphone as close as you can to your actor's mouth without seeing it in the shot.

Another good tip is to capture **natural sounds,** or sound effects that occur naturally during the scene. This may be something like a faucet turning on, or stairs squeaking, or birds chirping. If you're in a setting that has some type of atmospheric noise you'll want to capture that on it's own and later place it in the scene so everything feels like it takes place in that same setting.

Be careful with screaming or loud sounds. If something gets too loud, audio will **peak**, or clip itself off, creating an electrical, annoying, unprofessional sound. Most microphones can handle a good amount of loud noise, but keep an eye on it, especially if you're going from quiet to really loud. If your scream peaks and gets muffled or electrical-sounding, turn the microphone's sensitivity down and shoot the scene again. That way you'll have the volume turned up for the quiet portions, and turned down for the louder portions.

If you're recording narration or a voice over, find a quiet, small, non-echoey room. This way the sound doesn't bounce all over the place and sound like a cavern. You can even hang towels or blankets around a room, or create a blanket fort around your microphone and actor in order to dampen any distracting sounds. When capturing off-screen audio like this, ambient noise is your enemy. So dampen that "room tone" as much as you can and get good, clear audio.

A Few Words About the Set

You've heard the saying. *Location, location, location.* But once you've found your location, it has to look right. What's in the background is often as important as your subject. That includes colors, textures, and interesting things that jive with your story. You don't want to shoot a trailer for a 1920's book in a bar that looks like it's from "The Jetsons". You may have to **dress the set** to make it appear more appropriate.

This means planning to bring props, costumes, art, drapes, plants, and other decorative things to your shoot location. Intricate and beautiful sets can really improve your production value, and thus the effectiveness of the illusion you hope to create with your video.

When it comes to a convincing set, the devil is truly in the details. Be as meticulous as your patience (and the patience of others) allows. Even if you're choosing a background for a non-fiction trailer, try to find a backdrop for that interview that creates a sense of place or is somehow related to your subject or story.

This attention to detail is equally important for any costumes, props, or makeup. Take notice of what your characters would actually wear, and don't be afraid to show them with sweat stains, dirt, dried blood, makeup, styled hair, or whatever. Your goal should be realism when it comes to everything you're going to show on camera.

> **PRO TIP**: *Pay attention to your background colors, particularly the walls. Most of the time an apartment with white walls is incredibly boring. If you have a room with some color on the walls, painted window frames, or drapes, that immediately feels like a more textured, high-quality location.*

Production Value

Production value essentially means, "how expensive does it look"? Can the audience see the monster's zipper? Is the lighting any good? Are the camera angles interesting but easy enough to follow? This is one of the more subtle things that affects the way your audience feels about your video. Ever watch something and thought it looked "cheap"? Chances are you noticed the production value. Maybe it was poor lighting. Maybe the camera was tilted at an awkward angle in *every shot*. Maybe the lens was cheap, or foggy, or the effects weren't convincing.

This isn't to say you need to spend millions of dollars on lights and camera equipment. Production value also includes using what you have to your advantage. Do the backgrounds in your scenes look interesting, or are they just white walls? Most people won't notice these things, but will notice when they are absent.

Although production value mostly deals with things that happen while shooting, it can also become evident in the edit. Cheesy graphics or filters, bad music, or poor editing can all seriously hurt a video. However, for production, here are a few things to consider when shooting:

Light the scene properly. Harsh shadows (unless intentional) are frowned upon. Add back lights. Add eye lights. Make every shot look good and avoid it being "flat".

Pay attention to your camera angles and camera movement. Give your production some life by framing the shot properly! Remember the Rule of Thirds, and look up the 180 Degree Rule. You don't need a million dollar camera to make things look good. You just need some attention to detail.

Pay attention to what's in the background of your shot. Your apartment is boring. Find a location that is cool and has as much personality as your story! If you can't find one, make your location look like it has personality. Give it some art, colors, curtains, plants, anything to break up that ugly flat background space. And foreground space. Don't forget that.

Make sure your actors look the part. Their makeup and wardrobe needs to be as convincing as their acting. Take the time to consider what they would be wearing.

All of these things show through in a video, no matter how short, so pay attention when you're shooting and you'll be able to out-class any of your fellow authors.

Troubleshooting

No matter how good you are, the shoot will always have some sort of problem. Every shoot. Every time. Maybe the landlord will cut the water off in the middle of your rain scene (happened to me), or a construction truck will be parked on the sidewalk you intended to use (happened to me), or there's an international bike race running through your futuristic robot scene (almost happened to me). Who knows? The point is, things happen. Things break. People get sick. You've got to adapt to any situation, and keep your wits about you.

Before you go, I have a few more tips for you as you undertake the filming of your book trailer:

- Safety is paramount.

- If you need to get production insurance, do so.

- Things change. Adapt.

- Don't lose your cool.

- Be kind to people working with you.

- Filming takes a long time, be ready for it.

- Feed your people if you work them more than five hours. This is a golden rule of filmmaking. Even if you're not paying people, always feed them.

- Find interesting camera angles, and move the camera sometimes.

- Don't zoom. Please, oh please, leave this to the homemade disaster movies. It makes everyone else nauseous.

- Make sure your crew knows how much you appreciate and respect them.

- Make sure you've mastered your humble-brag for when you tell people you produced a book trailer. You want to look confident but not smug.

- Most importantly, have fun! If you're a creative author, most likely making a trailer will feel like yet another creative project. Enjoy it.

Finally, stick with your gut. If you've spent enough time in the planning stages, you should be ready to roll with the punches and capture some awesome footage.

Don't let your fear of embarrassment, or failure, or even lack of experience, get in the way of trying something amazing. The actual shoot is a combination of hard work and a lot of fun, so enjoy it. Experiment a little. Joke with people. Be inclusive.

People around the world willingly do this all the time, and they love every minute of it.

Post-Production: Where the Magic Happens...Again

Alrighty. The whole thing has been shot, and you've finally recovered from the massive hangover you wrought upon yourself during the wrap party. Now you've got to put it together. Easy, right?

Most likely you'll have this montage-ish, non-specific, artsy-type-thing, but the editing process is not exactly paint-by-number. You've now got all the right pieces; you just need to figure out how they fit together. To do this, you'll use an editing program to put together something pretty amazing. It all depends on *your* vision, though I encourage you to get more creative than a Power Point slideshow when it comes to assembling this bad boy.

Consider your audience. Think of what *you* would want to see were you watching someone else's video. Reassess the plans you made in preproduction. I'm willing to bet a lot's changed.

Don't assume your original idea is the best idea. Take an honest look at what you've got and see if there is a way to reimagine parts of it to pull out something more than what you put in. Think of this like the rewriting stage of writing a book. All the pieces are there, but are they the *right* pieces?

There are millions of ways to imagine and compose your video. No two trailers are alike, just like no two books are alike.

That being said, in order to make an effective video that's watchable and actually *helps* you sell books, there are a few guidelines to stick to.

The most basic way is to select clips from either your shoot, stock footage or photos, text, or graphic templates; edit them together into a montage, and pair them with music. Essentially, you make a music video out of your best shots. That's only the bare minimum, however, and no one likes it when you only do the bare minimum.

Dare to do something impressive. After all, doesn't your book deserve that?

Find an Editing Program

For some of you, this may be a non-issue if you've already found someone else willing to edit for you. Perhaps you're more of a lone wolf type, though, and intent on editing the project yourself. Who knows what you want more than you, after all? That's all fine and dandy, but what if you don't know *how to* edit?

I'm not talking about theory and technique. I'm talking about finding an editing program that you can use to actually do the work. It's unlikely you have a $50,000 editing suite in your basement. But fear not! Do not despair! You can find easy-to-use, cheap, or even free editing programs all over the place. Ain't the internet a wonder?

First, check to see if there isn't some type of video editor already installed on your computer, such as iMovie for Mac. There may be free apps out there as well for editing on your phone or tablet. Most likely, though, you'll want the ease of using a mouse and a computer. For that you can download free programs such as DaVinci Resolve (the free version), GoPro, Windows Movie Maker, Wondershare Filmora, VirtualDub, Avidemux, Zs4 Video Editor, and on and on and on.

I haven't personally tried many of these programs, so I can't vouch for them, and they're unlikely to be as versatile as the big three film-industry-standard video editing programs: Adobe Premiere, Avid, and Apple's Final Cut Pro.

If you're planning to make several videos, need a video software that's going to give you a vast array of tools, or simply want to do things more professionally, you may want to invest in one of those big three. According to my knowledge you have to pay for each of them, but costs have fallen like lead balloons in the last couple of years, and some companies even offer monthly subscriptions for around $20.

You may even be able to find computers at your local library or university library that have editing programs already installed. With a very little bit of research you can find something that works for you.

Even if you're lacking in time or motivation, but not money, you can always purchase editing services online. There are dozen of websites for finding freelancers or video editors who will bid on the opportunity to edit your video. These are sites such as freelancer.com, thumbtack.com, fiverr, elance, and even Craigslist.

There are even online build-by-template services that you can use, such as PowToon and Animoto and other, similar websites. These types of videos aren't overly customizable and I wouldn't consider using one of these services as truly "editing" your video, but their template may be all you need.

Once you've selected your editing software, don't freak out.

Most people aren't familiar with editing programs, and the layout can be strange. In some programs you might not even know what it is you're seeing at all! Take a moment. Do some breathing exercises. Drink some warm milk and relax.

Almost all video editing software requires a learning curve of some type. This is where, once again, the internet can come in handy. You can take classes at local schools, libraries, or from independent video editing teachers as well, but the vast majority of how-to editing knowledge can be found in video format, online. Youtube has hundreds and thousands of videos explaining how to do just about anything you can imagine, and there are more formal, structured teaching websites such as Lynda.com, Creativecow, or Skillshare. Even the software creators, such as Adobe (who created Premiere), have a beginner's course for editing that will walk you through the basic steps of getting to know the program so you're using all of the tools you need.

Spend some time getting to know your edit program. Play clips in slow motion and laugh at the deep-sounding voice. Play a clip backwards. Go to the color-picker and change the colors. Try out all of those cheesy filters. Put a little amateur text onto the screen. Play with it until you've gotten over the initial excitement of adding filters and goofing around, because if you don't, your final product will suffer for it.

PRO TIP: *The truth is, amateurs use too many filters, star transitions, and improper coloring all the time because they've never seen it before and they "just think it's so so so cool!" Professional videos don't use these things, or they use them subtly because the editors know that whatever pre-installed template your video program has, it's likely to be more than you need and look fake. Also, they're over it. They've probably played clips backwards in slow motion so many times that it simply has no entertainment value to them anymore. Instead, they'd rather create something beautiful, meaningful, and impactful. Strive to be like that.*

Editing

You've got your editing program, you've done your homework, and you've watched dozens of trailers that blow your socks off. Hopefully by now you've inferred how **absolutely essential** good editing is to a movie trailer. The same goes for your book trailer. Way back when I was still a humble post-production student, one of my editing professors constantly reminded us editing is the process of, "making chicken shit into chicken salad." This is true. Here are a few editing tips to help you do just that.

Setting up your Project

For the uninitiated, organization in editing is absolutely essential. Before you really get down to editing, take a few minutes to familiarize yourself with the workspace. Know where your bins are, where your sequences are, and where certain important buttons are, like the "cut" button or the "change clip volume" option.

You should be able to make **bins**, or folders, in your project where you can organize the different elements you'll be using such as footage, music, graphics, effects, and photos. I suggest you create a file structure that is easy and intuitive to understand. This will save you time later, and is important to familiarizing yourself with the project and setting it up in the way that best works.

You also want to make sure your footage is going to look its best, and will play back in the way it was intended. The best way to do this is to set up your timeline in such a way that the footage you captured with your camera matches the footage you see in your editor.

We've all seen those old videos that look stretched or squished. This error comes from footage that was shot one way and the editor—for some reason—tried to deliver it in another way. Often it's from a misunderstanding of aspect ratio or sequence settings or project settings.

For you, you probably shot in 1920x1080 High Definition at a 24 frames per second frame rate. You can verify this by looking at a clip or clips in your project window and making sure that's how it was shot. If it was not shot that way, no sweat. You'll simply set up your timeline to match your clip, however it was shot.

Most editing programs are drag-and-drop, so if you drag one clip into a new sequence or timeline, the timeline settings should match the clip perfectly. You can double-check this by finding the sequence settings, project settings, or timeline settings. You want to find an option that says something similar to "sequence matches clip settings." This means when you add footage to your timeline, it won't try to re-format your footage. You can change these settings if you know what you're doing or if you're looking for a certain look. If you're not as comfortable with editing, you probably want to stick with the default settings.

Start your Rough Cut

First, lay everything out in your timeline. Get a good idea of what goes where and how it will look. It's going to be rough, but most likely you're excited to see it starting to come together, so indulge yourself. Lay it out. Play around. Try out some music tracks. See it start to come to life.

Then find the rhythm. Yes, every edit has it's own pace and rhythm. You should be able to feel this when it's right, and it should bother you when it's not. Play it over and over, stare at it. Pick it out. Come back later and rewatch it. Start to feel it. Where does it give you goose bumps? Where do you find yourself getting bored? Editing is a little like sculpting, you just have to keep shaving away until you feel that it's right. You'll know you're striking the right chords when you can watch it over and over without losing interest. You should get to the point where you're proud of what you've put together, and can't wait to show it off. But wait. It's not ready just yet.

Editing to the Music

Having the right music can help you, but you don't always have to cut exactly on the beat of the music. Music can make the edits feel strong or impactful, but that may not be what you want. Maybe your story is slower and needs a cross-dissolve. It's all about feeling out what's right, and making the edit match those feelings. Think of it as visual poetry. It should flow. I'll talk a little more about music selection later, but for now, just consider how the right track(s) can make all the difference.

Continuity Editing

If you have any scenes that are continuous, **cut on the action**. This is a basic editing rule. It means if someone is doing something and you have two camera angles, cut from one angle to the next in the middle of their action.

For example, if your actor is opening a cabinet, you may want to cut from the first angle to the next halfway through the cabinet opening. This ties your two angles together by creating a sense of continuous time.

If you put together an entire scene like this so that the audience is seeing one continuous scene, it's called **continuity editing.** Typically, continuity editing is more useful for movies and short films, but every video is unique. You may have a story that is best set up in one scene. If that's the case, do some continuity editing to create a mini movie. Perhaps it's the intro scene to your novel, and it generates just the right kind of interest. I don't know how you'll want to approach your vision, but I want to provide you with enough information to know what your options are.

Shot Caller

Pick only powerful or meaningful shots. Don't use excessive footage just because it *looks nice*, in the same way you don't use big words when small ones will do.

Every shot counts, so use each effectively. For every single shot, you should be able to answer the questions, 'why that shot?' and, 'why there?' in the edit. If you can justify every cut, then you can be sure your video is tight and without unnecessary pieces. Editing video is like editing writing in this way, so heed the old adage, "murder your darlings."

Don't forget that sometimes less is more. You don't have to edit in a way that gives everything away. The human mind can pick things up that they've only seen in one or two frames. Use this effectively, especially when ramping up the action. You can shorten a fight scene to make it look more intense, or cut out some frivolous dialogue to make it move quicker and get to the point.

The feeling of your video should mimic the feeling of your book. Horror videos should be scary. Action videos should make you want to take over the world. Comedy videos should make you laugh. Even informational videos should have a little bit of drama and intrigue to them. This is as true for the edits themselves as for the content. Comedy videos tend to have longer shots, or complete sentences/scenes, while horror/action videos are much more likely to be fast-moving and jerky in the edit.

You can also mix and match shots. What I mean is you can take several lines/scenes from throughout your shoot or from different points in time in your book and cut them together to tell a complete, short, story. Just because the character doesn't say those words exactly in the book, or even during the shoot, doesn't mean you can't use their voice to help tell the story in the video! Use audio or shots that go together thematically to help tell the story or set up the conflict.

Goldilocks Length

As you refine your video, remember length is your enemy. Cut it shorter! You can tell a story in under ten seconds. Promise. Sometimes one shot can sum everything up. Sometimes ten different shots back-to-back can convey the feeling better than a line of dialogue. Don't be afraid to cut out anything that may be repetitive or not your best shot. Your audience is more likely to stay engaged if your video is short. They're even more likely to click on your video in the first place if it appears short enough.

To balance that, however, make sure you're getting across the information that you need to. Don't forget your script and those golden rules:

- Who is the main character?

- What does he/she want?
- What is standing in the way?

And for nonfiction:

- What problem exists?
- What or how does this book propose to solve/treat this problem?
- Why is this book different than other books of the same kind?
- What are the author's credentials?

It does you absolutely no good if you have a short, beautiful, well-scored, well-acted, well-shot video if no one knows what the story is about! Remember your audience doesn't know *anything* about your book, or even that it is a book, so be sure you're giving viewers what they need to know.

Creativity

You don't need to do this according to any given formula, though. Be creative with it. Remember that the most important part about your video is how the audience feels when it is over. How you portray any information is up to you. It is an art and it takes refining. Use your edits to create a feeling rather than worrying too much about the minutia. Build things up. Make creative edits. Have fun with it.

Stock Footage

Perhaps your video calls for an aerial of New York City, or you need a picture of something from World War II, or you're in need of a slow-motion clip of a bullet shooting through glass. If there are shots, or photographs, or even graphics that you're unable to create yourself, you may find what you're looking for by searching through **stock footage**.

Stock footage is footage, photos, graphics, music, and even sound effects that are royalty free and available to anyone to use (often for a price). You may even be familiar with the concept already because you've used a stock photo for your book cover or promotional material. If you're one of the uninitiated, prepare yourself. There are millions, tens of millions, even hundreds of millions of elements that you can search through in order to find what you're looking for. And they're typically high quality products made by professionals.

Use them to your advantage! That's what they're there for! Most of the time you'll use stock footage for one or two shots, such as a time-lapse shot of the sun setting over the Himalayas, but if you have the need and budget you can use stock elements for everything in your video. Even if you don't end up using them, you may be able to get inspiration from perusing through an online stock library.

Where to Find Stock

As with everything in the digital video age, there is an overwhelming supply of sources and suppliers of stock elements. A few of the top contenders as of the writing of this book, but by no means an exhaustive list, are istockphoto.com, pond5.com, market.envato.com, shutterstock.com, videoblocks.com, gettyimages.com, and on and on and on. They typically cost between $10 and $200 per clip, so keep in mind that stock can get expensive quickly.

Since you're using copyrighted work that someone else has created, you're actually paying to *license* your stock elements for a set amount of time or a certain type of use. Most stock sites have different licenses (and, accordingly, different prices) that you'll need to consider before purchasing. Be realistic about the license you need, because unless you're *actually* going to broadcast the footage on television, you probably don't need to pay for a TV Broadcast license.

Besides, if you do decide to go the TV route later, you can probably update the license at that time.

The Problem with Generics

The only real disadvantage to stock elements—other than missing out on the joy of creating these elements yourself, of course—is that many people can tell the difference between stock video and custom video.

In some cases, the difference in quality will be glaringly obvious, but in other cases the content itself will ruin the illusion because stock footage is intentionally generic. This means any clips you use will, of course, be generic. This is a matter of taste, requirement, and style, so it's nothing to lose sleep over but rather just something to be aware of. As with everything, use stock in moderation and keep it classy.

Music and Audio

The most valuable tip I can give you for editing is to place an incredible amount of importance on the audio. Music is what drives a story; it is the closest thing to a physical manifestation of an emotion. Make sure you find the right emotion, and use it well. Search the internet for hours to find the right music, and keep trying different tracks until you find exactly what you need.

Maybe you need several musical cuts. Most movie trailers use three (it's not a hard and fast rule, just an observation). Why? Because the mood of any piece should change (hook, build, bang!) and the music helps to guide that change. Combining several songs and sound effects together creates the mood, and that mood changes as you move through your story arch. The musical selection is often the difference between a powerful video and something only your Great Aunt Mildred would like.

Editing Music

Music will drive your video 95% of the time. Intelligent lack of music can do the same. When you're incorporating music, don't just slap it down and edit to the beat. Edit the music too!

Find the parts in the song that emotionally match the parts of your story and play those up. Edit the slow parts out. Cut and paste and match the music so it starts at the beginning of your trailer and actually ends at the end. Many times people will just fade the music out, and that's a sure sign of lazy, low-rent editing.

And please, **only use music you have the rights to use**. I doubt you paid Lady Gaga to license her song for your book trailer. It'll get flagged for copyright infringement if you choose to use it without permission.

Even if you can get away with it, using a recognizable song can work against you. Understand that using popular music—like a song you've heard on the radio—in a video often backfires unless it's a teenager/pop/YA type product you're advertising for. Popular songs date the video—and the creator. Try to avoid it, even if you do have the rights.

Other Audio

Not all audio is music. This includes sound effects, drones, screeches, and dialogue/sound bites/voice over. These elements can be used in conjunction with and just as effectively as the music. Use your audio clips to drive your video forward and to explain what's going on.

Keep your sound bites short and effective, but try to avoid making them cheesy one-liners or clichés (such as *"get to the chopper!"* or my favorite, *"in a world…"*). A horror trailer that makes you laugh because the sound bite is stupid is not effective.

Use sound effects and other audio to enhance the mood of the scene. For instance, if your video ends with a big bang or a big reveal, there's no reason you can't put a subtle "rising drone" noise underneath everything to ramp up the intensity, then follow it up with a loud drum hit. Just remember to use silence as effectively as sound effects.

Speaking of sound effects, don't underestimate them. Adding in a few well-placed sword swishes, whooshes, zaps, or pings can really up your game. Even without music, a good soundtrack keeps the tension where you want it and sucks the viewer in. These sound effects should be strong enough that your video feels empty without them, but subtle enough that a casual viewer doesn't know you used sound effects—in fact, they don't even *think* about the sound effects. They're focusing on the story. *That* is your overall goal.

Where to Find Audio

There are dozens of online resources for finding **royalty-free** music, or music that you can use or purchase without getting into major licensing issues. Many of these are the same stock sites where you can purchase footage.

You can easily find music tracks and sound effects designed specifically for trailers; music tracks that fit just about any mood you're going for. There are epic trailers, mystical fairy tales, ghostly horror tracks, sappy love songs, even porn-style music.

A quick internet search for "royalty free music" should turn up a number of online databases that you can search for your particular flavor, and their prices range from free all the way up to thousands of dollars.

Composers

But you don't have to use ye olde internet if you're not inclined to do so. Just like finding film professionals to help you during the shoot, you may be able to find folks out there willing to accept money, barter, credit, reels, or meals in order to score your video. These people can range from full-blown orchestral composers to audio technicians with a setup on their laptop. You can hit up local bands or friends who you know play music exceptionally well. If you're so inclined, try your own hand at composing using programs such as Garage Band, Soundtrack Pro, Audition, Protools, or a variety of others.

Public Domain

If you're not musically inclined and your budget is completely bottomed out, you can search for music tracks that are in the public domain. These are typically classical compositions and older songs (we're talking like 1920's old). Be careful with these, as sometimes the song may be public domain, but that particular performance may be under copyright with the performer or composer. If you're looking for a little Beethoven or Mozart, though, you can usually find a completely free recording to make use of.

Graphics

Now you have all of the images and sounds for your book trailer, but most likely that's not enough. You need something that's a little more elegant, ties the piece together, and, you know, actually *shows people the title of your book*. I'm talking here about graphics, and more specifically text graphics or titles.

In the past, a strong, smoky, grumbling voice narrated most movie trailers. A typical trailer usually started off with that all-too-familiar saying, "In a world…" and proceeded to highlight key phrases and plot points that would make audiences feel like they had to see the movie. Most of you can probably recite a generic movie trailer by heart. It goes something like this:

"In a world where choice is outlawed and nothing is free, one woman must face her darkest fears. She'll have to make a choice that changes everything. Even if it makes her an outlaw. This summer, join the adventure. Jane

Doe stars in **OUTLAWED FREEDOM II: THE SEQUEL.**"

Sounds kinda outdated, right? Nowadays that smoky-voiced narrator is more often than not replaced by large animated text that appears on screen with sound effects. These graphic text titles are used to sew the story together and drive home the main point of any video: the who, what, and why. These graphics also include quotes, reviews, poems, or anything that can't be physically filmed.

Watch any movie trailer. Or TV promo. Or commercial. Graphics are *everywhere.* And they're an excellent tool for creating gripping trailers.

Graphics and text can be so effective in a video that you can get away with text-only videos. That's essentially what kinetic typography is. But before you do this, consider how good your graphics actually look. Embrace your limitations if you can't do exploding 3D text that looks amazing. Find a more creative way to use what you can do and make it look sleek. There is no shame in black text on white as long as you use it effectively…like Apple does.

CGI

We also use graphics to create computer-generated images (CGI) such as the dinos in *Jurassic Park* and the exploding cities in pretty much every apocalyptic movie ever. CGI can be subtle changes like background replacement, or entire characters that don't actually exist in real life, like a Transformer robot. If you have the means and ability to create graphics on a 3D character-level like that, you probably don't need to read this chapter. Most videos, however, don't call for such a high level of animation, so for our purposes we're going to be mostly talking about text graphics and basic things like obscure backgrounds, title animations, and adding in your book cover.

Creating Titles

Whatever type of book trailer you're creating, you want to include at least some type of graphic. To do this, most video editing software has basic title-creation abilities. If you can, however, I suggest using a graphics program that is specifically designed for video such as Adobe After Effects or Apple's Motion. You can also design graphic elements with programs like Photoshop and Illustrator and animate them with a variety of other programs.

> **PRO TIP**: *For logos, try searching for images with a "transparent background," a "vector image," or even "logo png". These transparent backgrounds allow you to drag-and-drop the logo over your footage. No need for advanced graphic tools.*

But the program you use doesn't matter as much as how you use it. That's why I'm sharing some basic suggestions for how to take your on-screen text from black-and-white boring to something engaging and beautiful in its own right.

A Font of Knowledge

First, your font is important. The font should likely match the font of your book cover or be somehow associated or related to the look and feel of your book. We're still all about brand recognition here, and if your book cover has a certain look, color, and font to it, don't you think the commercial for that book should include the same? I think so.

Yes, there are exceptions to every rule. No, you're not that exception.

Whatever you choose for your font, make it good. Don't just go for what's easily available on your computer. Look up some new fonts by searching the internet for…you guessed it…free fonts. There are great, free resources out there for you to download original fonts, so there's no need to stick with Times or Arial. Varying the size, capitalization, and thickness can also make your text pop a little bit. Maybe make one word bold and another not bold. Maybe your book is called un**Bold**. See what I did there?

They're easy to install with one or two clicks, and a unique font gives your work a unique, professional quality. At least try to avoid the dumb fonts like that permanent marker font or Chalkboard or Papyrus.

PRO TIP: *No one will take your seriously if you use Papyrus. No one.*

Avoid bouncy letters and motions. It might be cute to you, but it looks terrible to everyone else. Most of the time the best way to introduce some text or graphic element is to *fade in* and *fade out*. You can do some subtle blur effect or even have it fly in from off screen, but I don't recommend doing any more than that. And please, oh please, if you're going to use some type of flying text or whatever, make sure the motion is consistent. There are very few things less professional than plain text floating in from all directions with no rhyme or reason.

Text Companions

Other things to consider are textures, background elements, strokes and gradients, and even solid colors. Plain text is boring, so do something that makes your graphic text look original. Plain black backgrounds are boring, too. Give your piece some drama with a subtle splash of color and a radial gradient in the background. Or a textured background, such as a rocky, cracked, or cardstock paper texture.

Brand Consistency

If you were smart, you had a professional design your book cover. Ask them to provide you with the font and colors they used, and keep your video graphics consistent with your book cover text.

Keep your text consistent throughout the whole video, too, by avoiding fonts that don't go together. Most of the time it's best to use the same font throughout, although there are times when mixing and matching is appropriate. But always, always know your reasons for switching fonts, font sizes, or colors.

Placement

Where you put your graphics is important, too. The rule of thirds still applies, and **balance** is important to consider. Words and images on screen have weight, and it is important to make sure the space is divided evenly. Either make things symmetrical or make sure the text is balanced in some way. Slightly off-center text is a sure mark of the uninitiated amateur.

Endpage

Even if you don't want any words on the screen for the majority of your video, you'll at least want some type of ending screen. You want to end with your CTA; text that lets the audience know the **name of your book**, **where they can find it, when it is available,** and probably your **author website**. This text typically belongs with that other all-important part of the ending screen: an image of your book's cover.

Find a way to incorporate the cover, whether it's just the cover photo on a black background, or if you can find a way to slap it onto a 3D book image, or simply place the image over a pleasing background with other pertinent information in it. You want to make it the easiest thing in the world for people to recognize your book and purchase it at any moment. If you do nothing else, you still need to have the title and some indication of where a person can get the book.

Oh, and if it's not already obvious, you should probably let your audience know that you're selling a **book**, not a movie.

And check the spelling!

Text is not the only graphic element you can use in a video. You can use fancy flourishes or swishes or even create an entire graphical trailer. There are some awesome things you can do with graphics that help to tell your story. Be creative, but keep it classy. Remember that simpler is better, especially if you're new to graphic design.

Important Things to Consider

Now that you've put it all together and are ready to output your completed video, take into account these few last-minute thoughts.

- Dummy-check your edit. This means make sure all of the lip-synching is on, all of the music is the right level, and all of the shots are there.

- Make sure your book title is legible and prominent. I'd hate for you to have an excellent video but a terrible title that no one can read!

- Make sure the video accomplishes what it should. Did you remember your CTA? Where someone can find more information? Is the author's name included? Can a person who sees the video easily figure out where they can buy or view the book?

- Check your levels. Make sure the sound is between -12dB and -6dB and that the colors are showing properly. This is more of a consideration if you're exporting for television, but simply looking at your work on another computer can change your impression of it. What you see and hear on your computer may not be what other people see and hear.

- Double-check all spelling, grammar, and font consistencies.

- Check the beginning and the end to make sure the video starts and ends in the right place.

- Make sure you have the right logos.

- Have someone else watch and critique. Hopefully they can spot any issues you have or stop you before you make any boneheaded moves. I once spent an enormous amount of time editing footage that was shot upside down. I had to turn everything back the right way, but my mind had gotten so used to seeing the footage flipped that I needed someone else to watch the program just to tell me if every clip was right side up! It seems simple, but having another person get fresh eyes on your piece may make all the difference in the world.

- Shorten it. It can always be shortened. Murder your darlings. Kill them dead. The shorter your trailer, the more likely people are to watch it. See how many times you can cut off five more seconds until it doesn't make sense.

- Let it breathe. Once you've finished, take some time to let it settle. Go for a walk. Sleep off the three energy drinks you've chugged. Think about something else for a while. Then come back to it with a fresh set of eyes and see if it's really as good as you thought. Chances are you can make it better.

- Know when it is done. Just as important as tweaking is knowing when to stop tweaking. Art is never finished, it is only abandoned, and your trailer is art.

- Be proud of yourself. Creating anything is hard, and critiquing something is easy. That's why there are so many more critics than creators. But steel yourself for any negative comments and stand up for yourself. You've just accomplished something incredibly difficult, taxing, risky, and quite possibly expensive. Take pride in your work.

Delivering: Sharing the Magic

It's time to get this puppy out in front of audiences. You'll need to go through a process called *exporting* (or *sharing* in some cases) in order to deliver your final piece to audiences. Basically what you're doing is telling the computer to take all of the separate information in your edit system and spit out one completed file. If you were cooking, think of exporting as the part where you bake all of the ingredients together. When it comes out of the oven, it's one meal ready to eat. So, too, with exporting.

Export Specifications Explained

Go to your video editor, select your timeline (where all of the clips are that make up your video), and go to **file→export** (sometimes called "**share**"). Look at all of the options and breathe. Just breathe. It is very confusing and scary to see all of those exporting options, so let me simplify.

Most likely you're trying to get your video on to YouTube or Vimeo or Facebook, yes? Most editing programs today have built-in settings for social media platforms like these, and it may be as simple as selecting "export to YouTube". If that's the case, then you're set.

Sometimes there will be options based on what type of video settings you have, such as "YouTube 720p" and "YouTube 1080p" and "YouTube 4K". These numbers represent the type of footage and size you would like to output, and that depends on the type of footage you've input.

If you followed our earlier recommendation, you've shot and edited in 1920x1080 high definition. If so, export 1080. If shot in 4K, then export 4K. Your goal is to find the type of file that is the same size as your footage. If you shot in a smaller format, such as 720, then *don't try to export it as a bigger file.* You can scale big footage down, but you should not scale it up.

> **PRO TIP**: *For best results, export according to your lowest common denominator. So if you have 4K footage, 1080 footage, and 720 footage, the video will likely look sharpest exported at 720. Unless you only have one or two 720 shots, then just scale those up to 1080.*

Say you need a different type of video file, or your video editing program does not have a YouTube or Vimeo setting. It most likely does have a "match settings" button, or you should have a pretty good idea of what type of file you want (like a .mov or a .mp4). Most editing programs now try to make it as easy as possible to get your settings correct, so there may even be an "automatic" export setting. If you already know your settings, you can plug them in manually, too.

If you're not sure of the best settings for your export, view the settings in your editing timeline. This will give you information like the frame rate (23.97 or 24 or 29.97 or 30 or whatever), your aspect ratio (16x9…don't even bother with the others), pixels (3840 x 2160, 4096 x 2160, 1920x1080, 1280x720, etc.), and possibly other information about your video timeline.

When totally in doubt, ask the internet! Most of the video sharing websites and platforms have very clear specifications and easy-to-follow instructions. Every situation is different so I can't tell you exactly what you'll need, but rest assured that the information is out there and should be fairly simple to research.

Whatever file you export, ***save that file somewhere*** on your computer. Make a backup copy. Save the copy somewhere else entirely for safe keeping.

Peer Review

At this point you may want to upload the trailer to your favorite website and be done. But wait! I suggest you have a few people you trust watch it first and provide some gentle criticism. The more eyes you can get on it before releasing the video to the public, the better.

If you can, try to get the opinion of someone who doesn't know what your book is about. Ask them whether the trailer made them want to read it, or at least gave them an idea of what to expect from the book. Ask them if they honestly understood it. Make sure it works for the unacquainted.

Accept any criticism with grace, and actually listen to it. But just like having readers look at the second draft of your novel, take what others say with a grain of salt. Not all opinions are created equal—don't go out and completely redo the whole thing just because your second cousin thought your romantic comedy trailer didn't have enough aliens—but if everyone is trying to politely tell you they sort of lost interest halfway through, then that's a pretty good sign some revisions are in order.

Be patient and strive to get it right. It can be tedious at times, but in the end you'll be happier that your video was perfect, rather than just *good enough*.

And thank your critics. They don't have to watch and review your book video, so if they do, thank them rather than getting angry with them for their opinions. In the end it's your call, so if you disagree with someone's comments, thank them and simply don't make any changes. You don't win friends and influence people by being cruel or defensive.

Once you've gotten all the criticism you can stand and you're convinced that the darn thing is absolutely going-to-win-an-Oscar-perfect, upload it to your favorite video platform (or, you know, *every* video platform) and then verify that it looks, sounds, and speaks exactly how you want it to.

Once Uploaded

Now that your book trailer is made, reviewed, and revised, it's ready to premiere to the world. You'll need to use it for promoting the ever-loving heck out of your book, because if used right it will be one of the strongest weapons in your marketing and promotional arsenal. But the world's best book trailer won't get your book a single extra raised eyebrow if no one sees it.

In the last section of this book, we'll go over in-depth techniques and tricks to use this video—and all of your other marketing tactics—to actually help you sell books.

HOW TO SELL BOOKS USING YOUR VIDEO

Your book is your baby. You've spent too much time, energy, blood, sweat, tears, and posture on it to simply shrug it off once it's complete. You want people to read it and love it, you want people to feel it as deeply as you do, to affect the world or be affected by the worlds you've created. For most of us, writing is a deeply personal endeavor, and it is intensely tied to our psyche. Sometimes more than we even want to acknowledge. Most writers don't appreciate putting so much work into their books only to remain unknown. We write books because we want people to *read* them, and, whether or not you like it, that usually means we need people to *buy* them, too.

In order to get the word out there that you have written a book that others *need to read*, those others have to have heard of it. This means most likely you will need to launch what I am going to call a ***marketing campaign***.

I know that phrase has a pretentious, ad-agency stigma etched into its insect-like carapace, but what I mean by a marketing campaign is simply a plan for how you will let the world know you have a book available. You have a product (your book), and everyone else is a potential customer. A marketing campaign is the toolbox that holds the various ways you will build yourself and your book a brand that communicates to customers your product is out there and readers need to be reading it.

Within this marketing campaign toolbox you have worlds of tools, which I encourage you to familiarize yourself with and eventually overwork until you've exhausted them. These are ways of spreading the word about your work, your expertise, your brand, or anything else you want your audiences to find. Tools including your social media presence, your email list, your blog, your website, your book cover, book tours and appearances, speaking engagements, print ads, e-magazine articles, brochures, television commercials, Youtube pre-rolls, Pandora ads, radio spots, website banners, mail pamphlets, even a door-to-door sales approach.

Think of all the ways presidential candidates try to invade your space and time in order to make you aware of who they are, what they stand for, and why you should vote for them. When a politician is campaigning, you better believe they're using every tool in that old toolbox to make you aware of them. I suggest you do the same with your book.

And so we come to this big, beautiful book trailer you've created. With all the work you've put into it, we can't let it die on the vine with only 12 Youtube views! We're going to use this incredible marketing tool to sell more books.

A Call to Action

So let's assume you've finished producing the absolute perfect epic book video. You couldn't be happier with the final product, it does everything you want it to, and it makes the hairs on your back stand up it's so freaking engaging. You've got it sitting on your computer desktop as a digital file, and you want to put it 'out there' for the world right this second because even the stodgiest anti-reading, troggle-headed, overly-critical doddering dolt will hurtle himself at the nearest bookstore upon only one viewing of this immaculately brilliant work of advertising and creative genius that is your book trailer. But how does said anti-reading troggle-headed overly-critical doddering dolt know which bookstore to hurtle himself into?

The first and most important thing a book trailer needs is *information about where to buy the book*. This may seem obvious, but it's surprisingly easy to forget that viewers need to know what to do after watching the trailer. You need to ask yourself, "what do I want viewers to *do*?" And you need an answer.

In marketing slang, that's what's known as the **CTA**, or **Call To Action**. If you've been reading along, this term should not be unfamiliar to you, as I've mentioned this several times before because it is so important. Your CTA is your knockout punch—it absolutely must be there in order to win.

The question your book trailer should answer is, "now what?" Your Call to Action is that answer. It should tell viewers where to find the book and what to do with that book. It can be as simple as "CLICK HERE TO BUY" or "READ IT NOW".

You want this CTA to be declarative and strong. Remember it is a call to *action*, so use active words. "Buy," "purchase," "get," "run, don't walk," etc. You should provide viewers **one** clear, easy-to-understand action to take. Just one. Anything more and people are less likely to do anything at all, because they feel the directions may be complicated. Simplicity is your friend.

You'll also want to make an idiot-proof indication of where or how someone should take that next step. This typically includes a link to your website, blog, online book-seller (for instance your Amazon page), or at the very least the name of the physical book store that our doddering dolt can hurtle himself towards.

For example, a complete call to action may look like, "Click this link to buy now on Amazon." Or "Get your copy on October 31st at Bill's Book Bargain on Broad Street." Or "Sign up here and join the movement."

The goal here is to make it as easy as possible for someone to watch the video and immediately purchase the book. The more clicks or steps from trailer to retailer, the more potential customers you're going to lose. If you're selling online (and there is absolutely NO EXCUSE for not selling online), you should have a clear, clickable link **IN THE VIDEO** that a viewer can click on. In most cases, this should take the viewer directly to the sales page for your book on your website or on a website like Amazon.com, iBooks, Barnes & Noble eBooks, Sony Reader Store, or other major ebook retailer. By having a direct link to the sales page for your book, a viewer can impulse-buy your book the instant they finish the video.

> **PRO TIP**: *If your website doesn't directly sell the book, but has a link to an external sales page like Amazon, you're complicating things for your viewer by adding an extra click—which means you'll lose a significant portion of impulse buyers. The harder it is to get to that "buy" button, the fewer people will click it.*

What I mean by "sell directly" is that the sales page for your book on your website has a "buy" button. Someone can click that button, and receive the book. It doesn't take them to another page, doesn't redirect them, doesn't connect to another page on your website, doesn't pass go or collect $200. It simply lets the person *buy the book right there*. If your website's sales page links to another page where that 'buy' button is, then put the link to *that page* in your video.

Although you should absolutely be selling online, the universe is a big place and I'm sure it contains at least a few reasonable exceptions or explanations for why you may not want to sell online. This may be something like you're only selling a special edition in person at a local venue, or your book is non-traditional and cannot be sold online for e-readers, or is only available at a certain event. Whatever the plan is, if you're not selling online, your trailer should include simple, accurate information about **where** *someone can purchase the book*. This may be the address of a local bookshop, or a link to the writing conference where you'll be signing and selling the limited edition, or whatever.

Less important but still useful is to somewhere in the video include a link to your website/blog/social media about you and your writing, especially for people who need more information. You should also include information about the event, such as a link to the conference promoter's website.

> **PRO TIP:** *If you're linking to a special event, see if the venue will return the favor and link to your book page as a form of cross-promotion.*

Where to Post

Alrighty. You've got all of the information communicated within your video, and people can link to the sales page. But no one is watching the thing. Why not?

Most content creators are under the assumption that "if you build it, they will come." This is not true with online video, especially if you're not already famous. There is no 'set it and forget it' option unless you've already built an **online platform** (I'm sure over the course of your writing career you've come to despise this term as much as I have) that more or less guarantees thousands of views. If you already have developed said platform, then you probably don't need to read this section.

For the rest of us, posting a trailer to Youtube and then walking away is going to garner about as much interest as stapling your business card to the wall at your local coffee shop. Maybe someone will pick it up, call you, and offer you lots of money. Or maybe tomorrow's lunar eclipse will give you x-ray vision. It's possible, I guess, but pretty unlikely.

The first thing to consider is where you will be posting your trailer and where that post is likely to intersect with viewers who would already be interested in reading a book like yours. This is where the trailer merges with the rest of your marketing campaign, and your overall brand as an author.

My recommendation, if you have no other plan, is to do as follows. Post the video to Youtube, Vimeo, or a similar video streaming/hosting service. Youtube is probably the best simply because it's the most well-known, it gets the most traffic, and it is the easiest to share and embed. There's no harm in using another service, I'm just saying for the sake of simplicity you are most likely to be familiar with Youtube.

Once the video is posted—in other words Youtube is **hosting** the video—you can then incorporate that into other parts of your online world. This means you should **embed** it in your website and in your emails that go out to subscribers. That way every time someone views the video—no matter where they view the video or how they got the link—they're seeing the version hosted by Youtube, adding to your view count and statistics.

Think of the Youtube as a one-room house where your video lives, the video itself is a couch, and each time you embed the video, you're creating a window to look into the house from the outside. Sure, someone may be watching the video as a link in your email newsletter, but they're still seeing the file as it exists on YouTube—much in the same way as if they're looking through the South window, they're still seeing the same couch as if they're looking through the North window.

In the same way you wouldn't want to put identical couches in different houses, you don't want to host the video in different places simply because it gets confusing for people searching for your video. Simpler is better, and you want the project to be streamlined. If someone watches your trailer, they should be watching the one single instance of that trailer.

Now that you have your hosting platform—in our example, YouTube, although Vimeo and other platforms work incredibly similarly—you want to optimize your video for success.

Posting Tips

A wise author knows all about titling, keywording, tagging, and creating hyperlinks to their work and their website—and you're a wise author. Treat the video as if it were your only communication with the outside world.

Be sure your title is attention-grabbing, clear, and easy to remember. Obscure or long, involved titles are harder to remember and search for. If someone were recommending the book to a friend but couldn't quite remember the title, try to think of what they'd search for. This will help people find you. The title **Book-Video_version4_March152019** isn't going to be easy to find. "**Stupid Little Brat by John Doe – Book Trailer**" is going to be a lot more finder-friendly. A good title will also help increase your **search** *engine optimization* (SEO) and help your video appear hire in search rankings.

Improving SEO is the practice of making it easy for someone who doesn't know your book is out there to find it. This includes adding keywords that your target audience may be searching. It includes linking to relevant topics and articles. It includes an internal consistency across different websites. Very basically, your title and your keywords should make a logical sort of sense. So, for example, if you've written a detective novel in space, it makes sense that people looking to read detective novels set in space should be able to use a search engine (i.e. "Google it"), and find your book.

For more information on SEO tips and tricks, you'll have to do a little bit of research to find much more complete sources of information.

Most video players, including Youtube, have a description section for '*More Information*' where the person who uploaded the video (you) can add in, well, more information. Don't ignore this section.

Provide every bit of information you can in the description and other information around where the book trailer will play. This will increase your SEO, help you favorably within the algorithm, and is an excellent spot to place valuable information. In the description, you'll want to include a (short) description of the plot, a link to your author website, your Facebook page, the Amazon store where the book can be purchased, your publisher's website, how to subscribe to your email list, relevant links to other books or projects you've completed, credits, or other identifying information.

Try to think of anything that a viewer who knows *nothing about you* would want to know if they're a little bit interested. This information should help persuade people to take the next step, whether it be to find out more information about the topic, or go straight to the sales page. And even though the link is in the video, *put a link to the sales page in the More Information area, too.*

On some video platforms you can even put links right on top of the video itself, so a person can simply click the screen and land on your sales page. Since we're all about selling your book, keep in mind that you want to offer viewers the fewest clicks from your video to the "buy" button. It's all about ease. The easier it is for people to get to your book, the more likely they are to buy.

Oh, and check the writing in all of your descriptions! No one will believe you're an excellent writer if your description section is poorly written, misspelled, or looks like that sketchy email claiming to be from a Ugandan prince.

Thumbnails

Be sure to select a relevant and exciting image to appear as your thumbnail. This is the image that will appear when someone searches for your video or when it shows up in a list with other videos. Usually more interesting, exciting, or sexy thumbnails garner more clicks.

I recommend *against* using "click bait", such as a picture of girls in bikinis for your sci-fi book about space slugs. This is because click bait actually works against you, as viewers will purposely *not* buy your book or recommend it if they feel they have been lied to or lured in by false promises. And the internet can be a dangerous place if commenters think you're scamming them.

If, however, your trailer does involve something enticing, exciting, or intriguing, you should definitely include that in your thumbnail. When in doubt, use your book cover, or at least incorporate the book cover into the thumbnail.

Keywords

Use as many **keywords** as you can in your description and in the metadata when uploading a video. Search engine algorithms change all the time and statisticians and online gurus are constantly analyzing and pontificating the current and most useful ways to use keywords to maximize SEO. If you're really into it, you can adapt to the times. When in doubt, stick to clear, classy keywords that are descriptive, unique, and search-friendly.

Most keywords are "under the hood," or invisible to the casual viewer. With YouTube and other video platforms there are options to add keywords when uploading the video, which you can always go back and add to or change later. Some platforms have a limit on the number of keywords, so I would say use as many as they'll let you.

You can also integrate keywords into your descriptions or *More Information* boxes, but be sure those keywords are organically woven into the description, not just a laundry list of words. If YouTube or Google thinks you're trying to keyword-load, you may actually be punished in the algorithm and not appear in search results. This is because YouTube, Google, and other search engines frown upon trying to game the system—ideally if your content is good enough, people will see it. Your descriptions should be adding value and understanding to readers, not stuffed with keyword non-sequiturs for SEO purposes.

Channel Appearance

Finally, make sure your channel is up to snuff. This means your picture is up there, there is information about you, your work, and your philosophy (why someone should subscribe and follow you), and there are links to outside sources like your website or Kindle profile page. Nothing looks spammy, incomplete, or unprofessional. Your channel is another extension of your brand, so make sure it is presentable to potential buyers. It also means deleting all of those old videos that you wouldn't want the world to see.

If you'd like to keep personal videos separate from professional videos (like book videos), then create two channels: one for personal stuff, and another, more professional channel for yourself as an author. Only post writing-related and author-related information to your professional channel.

You want your media and messaging to be consistent throughout your internet ecosystem making it easy for potential viewers/readers/followers to navigate and understand. If you have a different channel for every writing-related post, or if you are mixing and matching personal and professional, potential customers get confused, start to think you're unprofessional, or may simply not know where to go next. Streamlined user experience is the name of the game, so keep it clean, simple, and relevant.

Remember, everything about your book video and online presence should make things easier for audiences to find and buy your book. Make it easy enough that your illiterate, half-blind, computer-ignorant Great Aunt Ethel could figure out where to click to buy. That's your purpose.

How to Promote

Now that your video is out there, your channel is up to snuff, and everything looks good, it's time to really explore avenues of promoting your video—and by extension, your book.

Most of you will be self-promoting, and won't have multimillion-dollar budgets that can be divvied out by advertising gurus. All of the promotion of your book is on you, my friend, and the first thing you're probably thinking is that in order to get the word out, you need to get that video everywhere you can online.

Anywhere you would mention your book, drop in a chance to show folks the video. In addition to all of the avenues that you're probably already pursuing, try tagging. Posting. Re-posting. Tweeting. Sharing. Cross-promoting. Blogging about the book. Blogging about the video. Blogging about the experience of creating the video. Put a link in your email signature. Talk about the book at parties. Or the grocery store. Mention it in all of your presentations. Tell coworkers. Have your parents or kids tell their friends. You can even go as far as bringing up a link on every desktop in your local computer class or Apple store, just hoping that someone will click and view (just don't get yourself in trouble!).

Get creative and think of as many ways to access audiences as you can. But don't let the sheer size of this step daunt you, because you don't have to do it all at once. The main thing to remember is that promoting your book and mentioning the video should come up organically. Get yourself into the mindset of bringing it up in any circumstance, and you'll find that simply keeping the book in the forefront of your thoughts will make promoting feel easy and natural because it's what interests you! If you promote on one platform per day, or even just mention your book once per day, you'll find that your efforts become exponential.

Online Promotions

One of the most useful avenues for promoting your book is going to be the internet.

If you're with me so far, this probably isn't a shocker.

Specifically, let's talk about how and where to put your book trailer for free that will get it noticed, and then drive viewers back to your book. The most important part of online promotion is to ensure you've made the process of buying your book as seamless as possible. You really want the process to feel effortless, idiot-proof, and ripe for impulse buying, and you do that primarily by limiting the number of clicks from trailer to purchase button.

Once that system is set up, it's just a matter of posting that video—and link—where people will see it.

Online, a few of the most common free places to post are YouTube, Vimeo, Facebook, Twitter, Instagram, Pinterest, Reddit, Amazon and other sales sites (wherever you can), Goodreads, Librarything, LinkedIn, Meetup groups about writing (or video production), and any and all large public platforms that allow you to post for free. Remember, though, there is no such thing as, "if you post it, they will come," so you have to focus on engaging audiences and being an active member on whatever platforms you choose.

Being an active member doesn't just mean responding to comments on your own work. You've got to locate and connect with small, related communities online. If you're an avid Facebook user, most likely you have access to online communities that share similar interests through your groups. There may be a writer's group, a group focused on your book's genre or related topics, or professional groups you're already a member of who would be more than happy to check out your book trailer. Anywhere you can promote your trailer that will get people to watch it—especially people you don't already know—is going to help build your views and spread your message.

This can seem overwhelming, especially at first, but there's a secret. Pick the one or two sites you already use and engage with most often, the ones you really enjoy using, and focus your efforts there. Everything else you can update almost as an afterthought, but if you're focusing your attention on sites you'd be using anyway, you're more likely to look authentic and keep promoting and engaging. If *you're* interested, then *audiences* are more interested. *That's* what will get others to share your work.

Engagement is also important because internet content has a shelf-life approximately on pace with a drop of water in the desert. The only way to stay relevant is to keep interacting with your content and your audience. Remember, each person is a potential reader, so give them something to keep exploring!

Aside from social media, you want to make the book video incredibly prominent—even featured—on your website, your blog, and your own online accounts. You can then promote the trailer on other blogs or channels by guest-writing, making guest appearances or showing up as an expert in other people's YouTube videos, or contacting other wide ranging websites or e-zines and offering to write a guest blog or be a featured book trailer/author/expert.

This isn't likely to work for free if you're contacting a national news outlet or a huge national corporation, but there may be a local newspaper, magazine, business section, or media magazine that is starving for interesting content that would be willing to write a story on you and your trailer or your book.

PRO TIP: *As you're looking for people to leave reviews about your book, you may be able to entice them by showing off your book trailer. OR vice-versa: try to promote your book trailer and if they seem interested, ask if they'd throw in a review.*

You should also contact your local writing groups to see if they have suggestions on where you can promote locally, or if they will mention you in their newsletter or other outreach.

You never know who is looking for a story about a good book or a good book trailer, and you never know which social media site is going to bring you the most eyeballs. Just remember that **engagement is key**.

Email Newsletter Promotions

One of your biggest promotional tools is likely your email newsletter and your subscribers. If you're building a community through a newsletter—weekly, monthly, annually, whatever—then that newsletter is situated to deliver valuable content to its readers. What could be more valuable and interesting than a new book trailer for your upcoming book? This is a great way to generate buzz, get honest reactions, and simultaneously promote the book, a book launch, a signing event, or anything else. It's perfect because a book trailer is real, valuable content that is interesting to your subscribers.

And the content you provide doesn't just have to be the book trailer itself. Maybe in the weeks before you're going to release the trailer you release behind-the-scenes videos or photos, or expert interviews, or teasers. Maybe you write a short article (or shoot more video!) talking about the experience of creating the book trailer. Your audience, fans, and other authors are likely to eat those stories right up.

Your newsletter is likely to be more popular and gain more subscribers if you are offering content to your readers. This means content other than the book trailer (you're likely running promotions, sales, and giveaways of all kinds in your newsletter already) that your fans find engaging. Your newsletter is your way to capitalize on all of the footage you've captured and all of the creative work you've done for your book trailer.

Your book trailer isn't a one-off film shoot, either. Not if you don't want it to be. Milk it for all it's worth by filming extra content specifically for promoting over the long term. All of those extras and bonuses you can roll out over time through your newsletter.

For example, suppose we take our dinosaur fossil book from earlier. You've interviewed the world's top *pachycephalosaurus* expert, but of course only 30 seconds of that interview appears in your book trailer. You have a whole hour of great sound bites, though! Why not release those sound bites as separate content that you can share with your newsletter and on your YouTube channel to create a bigger library of interesting, meaningful content? You can turn one interview into ten different videos, and all of those videos are valuable, consumable content to the type of people most likely to buy your book.

In addition to your own newsletter, look into opportunities to be featured or advertise in other newsletters. These may be national writing or reading newsletters or subscription services, such as Shelf Awareness, Goodreads, or LibraryThing. They may be publishing companies that run newsletters about the industry and feature authors or books. They may be genre-specific communities, such as a true-crime newsletter or a YA-novel listserv.

Not all of these opportunities will be free, but if you can find a way to solve someone's problem or provide valuable content, you may find there are free ways in to even the most traditional pay-for-ads model. Alternately, we will talk about whether or not you should consider forking over a little dough to get your trailer—or book—featured in these newsletters. Once you do the math, spending may be the smartest way to go.

Physical Promotions

The internet is not the only place to show off your new book trailer. With a tablet, laptop, television screen, or even your phone, you can take your trailer on the road (it's a pun...get it?).

One of the best ways to get new fans and readers is through live, physical events. That means going to networking events, book signings at local book stores, writing conventions, and any other place where you can actually talk to real, actual people and get them to take a look at your trailer or hear about your book.

It doesn't have to be book-related events, either. You can set up a stand at local festivals, fairs, farmer's markets, or any other large public event where they allow venders to sell their wares. If you have a booth set up with your book (or books), passerby may stop in to ask what your book is about. But if your booth has a laptop set up playing your trailer on a loop, you're going to get at least twice as many people stopping by to watch the trailer, *then* ask about the book.

This is a bit of a psychological trick. First, moving images and flashing lights attract people at events. Secondly, people are more likely to watch the trailer because it is socially acceptable to learn about the book—quickly—without doing all of that awkward *talking to an actual person*. A book trailer they can watch very quickly helps people get comfortable with the idea, and it piques their interest, resulting in more traffic, more meaningful conversations and more sales.

Showing off your book trailer also works for convincing booksellers to sell copies of your books. Independent and local bookstores are approached by local authors fairly often, and there's no guarantee they'll be able to sell your book for you. If you're trying to convince them to carry your book, using your book trailer as a way to show off—very quickly—how great the book is can turn a "we're not interested" into a "yeah, we'll buy a few copies."

PRO TIP: *If it feels right, you may even suggest they run your trailer on a loop through the shop window, thus intriguing people to come into the store to check out some books. It's a win-win because it garners interest for the book shop in general and your book in particular. I don't suggest being pushy, but if your trailer is good enough, maybe you can work out a deal.*

You can use your book trailer anywhere you can sell books, so get creative. Have a friend who's in a band and you're sitting at their merchandise table? Throw up the trailer and a couple copies of your book. Know of a local film-festival going on? See if they'll run your trailer before the films and sell your book in the lobby. Going to a professional speaking event? Have your trailer running on a laptop next to your meet-and-greet table. The possibilities are limited only by your imagination.

Paid Promotions

Okay, so you've done all of the free and organic marketing and promoting you can think of, but you want something that can reach a broader audience. Video content (like your book trailer) is perfectly suited for this avenue as well. The trick is figuring out how you go about reaching those larger audiences.

This is where you have the opportunity to dip into broadcast work and other traditional advertising methods, as well as paid social media marketing. By that I mean you can use audio and video content to create online commercials, banners, print ads, radio spots, Pandora ads, Youtube pre-rolls, and even television commercials. These are typically pay-per-click ads, and likely involve spending a little bit of money. Sometimes a *lot* of money.

Now hold on just a second.

Before you freak out, I want to strongly, *strongly,* **STRONGLY** encourage you to do your research before forking over any amount of money to promote your work. Get to know what the local markets are, and whether spending the money on a broadcast commercial will actually provide you with dividends.

My father's favorite admonition when I was growing up was, "do the math." Make sure you do.

To illustrate the importance of adding it all up, let's try a thought experiment.

Do the Math

Say you're selling your book for $1 online. Your local television station is running a deal where you can have them play a 30-second commercial for $100. That commercial, according to the television station ratings, will reach a total of 10,000 people by the end of its run. Is it worth it to buy this commercial space?

At first you might think, *heck yes!*. If you're going to sell 10,000 books and only spend $100, then you'll have made a whopping $9,900. That's a really good return-on-investment. But before you imagine what you'll do with your newfound wealth, consider that not all 10,000 of those people will buy your book. The fact is many of them are probably watching TV because they don't want to read at all. So, of those 10,000, try to be realistic with your estimation of how many people will actually want to buy your book. And your estimation is almost always going to be more optimistic than the truth.

But let's be optimistic for a moment. Let's assume 10% of the viewers see your commercial and then follow it to your book's sales page. That's 1,000 people who click on your sales page. *But not all of them will buy the book.* In fact, again being optimistic, assume that 10% of those people actually buy the book. So, 100 people have made it from television commercial to final purchase. And that number decreases significantly with each additional click a buyer has to make.

Anyway, let's assume 100 buyers, which means you make $100. And you spent $100 to put your commercial on air, so it's a wash. Still worth it, right? Exposure and all of that. The more people read your book, the more people will recommend it. So it's still a win. Right? Right?

Except you forgot to factor in the cost of making the commercial, as well as the amount of hours you've spent getting the commercial from concept to television. If you look at it like that, you're most likely in for a bit of a loss.

This isn't to say traditional advertising is ineffective. In fact, it's known to be extremely effective—that's why it's so expensive—but only when the market research has been done. All I'm saying is do the math before forking over the dough.

Do a little bit of market research for your local area by looking up the type of people who watch television at a certain time, which shows are on, and if the viewer's demographic matches your book's demographic. Most television stations that will sell you ad space can provide this information, but don't always take a sales person's word for it.

More Paid Advertising

Okay, so you've done a bit of research, you want to invest some money in your marketing campaign, but don't know where to go. Your first stop should be opportunities that you can handle yourself. This includes creating ads for websites and video services like Youtube, Vimeo, Google, Facebook, Instagram, Pandora, and other websites and blogs. Most websites want commercials on their sites because *that's how they make money*. With a little bit of navigation suave, you should be able to locate that website's sales page, or at least a way to contact their sales team. You then follow the instructions from there.

For television commercials, radio spots, and other, larger broadcast opportunities, I'd say start locally. Most local news channels have some type of advertising sales wing, and they exist to do exactly what you're looking for:

put your commercial on the air. Each channel is likely to have a different demographic and pricing structure, but they are likely your first step into the media broadcast world. Some news stations or television stations can even help you with an online rollout and advertising campaign. And, since they're local, you can actually meet with a real, live person who can help guide you through the process.

In addition to a television station, you can search for certain industry professionals known as media buyers. Some of them work independently, and some work through advertising agencies. Media buyers are essentially brokers who buy advertising time and sell it to advertisers (you). They can place your commercial where you want, whether on television, radio, or print. Advertising agencies (sometimes with their own media buyers) can also place your commercials and provide plans for broadcasting your message, as well as analytics for how it works.

Most media buyers and advertising agencies work with very large accounts, such as big businesses and large organizations, so be aware they may not be willing to take on a single author unless that author really wants to pay through the nose.

With such a wide variety of services, the prices vary just as widely. Try to talk to a few sources to get an idea of how much money you may have to spend, and how much money you (realistically) stand to make by forking out that dough.

Each book is different, and requires an equally customized approach. There is no standard approach to your situation, and since technology changes daily, it would be impossible to cover every avenue of marketing strategies and advertising opportunities in this short book. Do your research, and try to have fun with it. You'll likely learn more about how our commercial landscape looks than you ever wanted to—and you might even find it as fascinating as I do.

AND FURTHERMORE: DON'T DO THESE THINGS!

You can do so many things in so many ways when it comes to video, and they would all be correct. The possibilities of how you use video to promote yourself are mostly endless, and I've done my share of telling you what you should do to capitalize on that. Now let's look at a few things you should *not* be doing when it comes to making a trailer, promo, commercial, or explainer video for your book.

The One Rule to Rule Them All

I'd like to draw your attention to the most important rule for authors: tell a good story.

Your video is not a substitute for your query letter, synopsis, sample chapters, or even as a showcase of your writing skills. But it is yet another way to tell a story, and that is ultimately what everyone wants to consume. All of the marketing, advertising, and content you create should first and foremost tell a good story. And everything you do should work together to tell a bigger, better story.

Your video can help to promote you. It can pull in new readers, intrigue audiences and agents alike, but it should be only part of the package. You still need to excel at traditional types of book promotion, especially if you're hoping to find an agent, editor, or publisher. At the end of the day, your video is a tool to get people to read your book. But the book should stand on its own merits.

The Other Rules

- Don't forget to include your name, the title of your book, where people can find it, and the sales link.

- Don't force people to watch your video. Entice them, tease them, and *ask* them, but a captive audience is unlikely to enjoy it.

- Don't create clickbait. For the uninitiated, **clickbait** is when the image or words describing your video are purposefully but deceptively attractive, even if your content is not.

- Don't monetize your video. Nothing is more annoying than having to watch a commercial before watching a commercial! It may seem tempting to try to gain every red cent you can from the video, but this may hurt you more than help you. Keep it clean and classy, and your readers will appreciate it. Realistically, the sales you lose aren't worth the .02 cents you make in Youtube royalties.

- Don't make your video too long. Remember, around the two-minute mark is a good place to be. Less is more. Brevity is the soul of wit. Make it shorter.

- Don't use work that isn't yours. If you haven't paid for it or gotten permission, then don't use it! Copyright infringement is just as bad as plagiarism and can get you into legal trouble quickly. You don't want to forfeit your book sales because you used Green Day's song without permission.

- Don't use offensive music or imagery. Use your discretion and be professional, even if your subject matter is a bit taboo. You can be scandalous and alluring, but avoid things that will turn viewers away. Things like pornography, too much gore, or excessive cursing are typically the worst culprits. Remember, you don't ever see a sex scene in a movie trailer.

- Don't make lazy edits. Every cut should count, every shot should be useful.

- Don't put it out there without letting someone else critique it first. Someone brutally honest who generally has good taste.

- Don't muddle your message or try to advertise for more than one book. Obviously the exception is if you have a series you're promoting, but if you think you can do the old two-birds-one-stone approach by making one video for two (or more) unrelated books, think again. Your message will get diluted and you'll lose potential readers to confusion.

- Don't assume viewers understand just because you do. People watching your video haven't read your book and can't read your mind. The message should be clear to everyone.

- Don't make things up, such as fictitious awards or quotes from critics. You may think it's cute, but it ain't. If you don't have relevant reviews or haven't won any real competitions, simply don't mention anything. Falsifying reactions to the book makes you seem illegitimate at best, criminally fraudulent at worst.

- Don't colorize your video too much, or make it too dark. Filters and overly-contrasty footage aren't just examples of poor editing, they're hard to see on some monitors.

- Don't ever imply a previous friend, author, employer, filmmaker, or associate of yours was unprofessional or dislikable in any way.

- Don't sweat the small stuff. It's easy to get lost in the details, so don't give yourself a stroke stressing out about your trailer. Take it easy. Be forgiving.

- Don't stop checking on it. Once you've uploaded it and started promoting it, don't just sit back and hope for the best. Track your hits, respond to comments, keep talking about it, and keep making sure it's in good working order.

- Don't forget to keep updating! Things go out of date quickly in the digital world. Re-cut your video and add to it when it starts to feel old. Replace it if you're no longer getting any use out of it. Make sure it stays relevant and trendy.

- Don't forget to enjoy it. 'Tis a great adventure you've undertaken. Cherish it.

SEEK PROFESSIONAL HELP

Not everyone was created with the visually artistic gene. We all need help from time to time, and maybe creating video isn't one of your particular strengths. Or maybe you don't have the time. Or the resources. Whatever the case may be, there's really no shame in seeking professional help.

I'm not saying you need to see the neighborhood psychiatrist and get your mind reconditioned using hypnotherapy to open yourself up to your artsy side. Rather, lean on the experts around you. If you have an internet connection or a resourceful friend, you can find a professional to help you. Sometimes you can even harness an entire production company to take your ideas and run with them. Your level of involvement is ultimately up to you, and if you don't think you're up to the task of creating what you need on your own, go see the experts.

Just like with everything in life, you don't have to face it alone.

HOW TO GET STARTED

Just like writing a book, the idea of making a book trailer seems both daunting and deceptively easy at the same time. But just like writing, create your video one chapter at a time.

Take your book. Write an exciting scene on one page. Turn that into a script. Adjust to taste. Repeat until you have it right. It all starts with the story. That's your opportunity to shine as a creative person. Remember that you're trying to convince people that you are a great writer, so write something great and show it off.

Your goal isn't necessarily just to sell books. If you're only in it for the money and don't have the passion, I don't imagine you'll stick with writing for too long. And I'd be shocked if you write a bestseller without trying. No, your goal is to create a way to get people invested in your story, in your characters, and to entertain and even impress audiences that may want to read your book. Not because you want money, but because *you've created something amazing.*

Make no mistake, writing a book is an accomplishment. Be proud of it. Show it off.

The final lesson is to never lose sight of what you're doing. Writing books, making videos, or creating anything at all should most importantly be fun. I think making your book trailer should be an adventure. It'll be tough at times, but it should always be enjoyable. It's a drug. Get hooked.

A friend of mine who works on films out in Hollywood ends all of his crew emails with a quote, and I believe it is the most appropriate thought to leave you with.

Sometimes this may feel like a job, but it's the best damn job in the world.

BEFORE YOU GO

This book is a self-published work, and my most treasured source of feedback is the reaction of my readers. I am honored that you've selected my work to read, that you've spent a few hours hearing my voice in your head as you've made your way through these guidelines. I encourage you to post some feedback, as that is your most direct line to me. Let me know what you thought, let me know how you felt, let me know if this was at all helpful. This is your chance to make this one-way conversation into a two-way dialogue. I would love to hear your thoughts, even if all you do is give me a few stars.

As the key audience for this book is likely to be self-published or e-published authors like myself, it's likely you know how important this feedback can be. Not only to the popularity and ranking of my work, but to my own self-assessments. Sometimes our work lives or dies based on the critiques of others, thus, if you've made it this far I am now at your mercy.

As with any creative work, I couldn't have done any of this alone. Thanks are always in order, and the following people deserve a special shout-out, whether it be for training me in writing, filmmaking, or simply prolonging my sanity. It would be impossible to thank everyone who has influenced me, and a few words in the acknowledgements section is a woefully inadequate thanks to all of you.

Notwithstanding, I would particularly like to acknowledge my parents, Richard and Annette, my brother Bryan and sister Melissa for their constant support, ideas, input, reviews and—yes—harsh criticism. They, as well as the rest of my extended family, have been a huge support in all of my creative works. It means the world to have so many people cheering me on.

The professors and educators throughout my scholastic and professional career have helped shape who I am and how I perform my work. Their influence is the foundation for my creative skills, and my gratitude for having them in my life cannot be overstated.

Thanks also to all of the film industry professionals I've had the pleasure to work with and learn from over the years, in particular John Woody, Bryan Woodward, Doug Bischoff, Pamela Justice Thornton, Patrick Bedall, Deven Langston, and many, many more. The greatest thing about the film industry is that it is also our passion. We are all constantly learning from each other.

In Richmond we have an incredible resource for authors, an organization known as the James River Writers, through which I have learned so much. In fact, they have helped inspire the writing of this very book. In particular, the friends I've made and the influencers I've followed through the JRW's events include Katharine Herndon, Kristie Tuck-Austin, Bill Blume, Kris Spisak, and everyone who supports the writers of Richmond, Virginia. I cannot overstate the impact they've had on me as a writer and as a member of the community.

Finally I'd like to thank you, dear reader. Without you, all my words are just symbols made of pixels, devoid of meaning or purpose. Keep reading, keep writing, and keep inspiring. I am forever grateful to you, and I never want you to forget it.

I sincerely hope I have helped in some small way, that I've encouraged you to take the first step, or the next step, or the last step in your journey. I wish you the best in your future endeavors.

Here's to you and a blinding bright future,

Richard
August 20th, 2016
Revised: December 24th, 2019

www.ingramcontent.com/pod-product-compliance
Lightning Source LLC
Chambersburg PA
CBHW020554220526
45463CB00006B/2297